Finding
Christ
in the
Book of Order

Finding Christ
in the
Book of Order

William E. Chapman

Witherspoon Press
Louisville, Kentucky

Unless otherwise noted, Scripture quotations are from the New Revised Standard Version of the Bible, copyright © 1989 by the Division of Christian Education of the National Council of the Churches of Christ in the U.S.A. Used by permission.

Quotations from the *Book of Order* and *The Book of Confessions* of the Presbyterian Church (U.S.A.) are used with permission of the Office of the General Assembly of the Presbyterian Church (U.S.A.).

Book interior by Michelle Vissing

Cover design by Jeanne Williams

First edition

Published by Witherspoon Press
Louisville, Kentucky

Web site address: www.pcusa.org/witherspoon

PRINTED IN THE UNITED STATES OF AMERICA

05 06 07 08 09 10 11—10 9 8 7 6 5 4 3 2

Library of Congress Cataloging-in-Publication Data

Chapman, William E., 1933–
    Finding Christ in the Book of order / by William E. Chapman.
        p. cm.
    Includes bibliographical references.
    ISBN 1-57153-042-8
    1. Presbyterian Church (U.S.A.) Book of order. 2. Presbyterian Church (U.S.A.)—Government. 3. Presbyterian Church (U.S.A.)—Rules and practice. I. Title.
BX8969.6.C47 2003
262'.05137—dc21

                                                                2003007932

Contents

Foreword

At a recent ecumenical meeting a colleague from another denomination asked me, "Who is the head of the Presbyterian Church (U.S.A.)?" She was somewhat surprised when I answered rather quickly, "For Presbyterians that is obvious from the very beginning of our *Book of Order.* Jesus Christ is the head of the church."

It is one of the strong and abiding commitments of the Presbyterian tradition that no person or institution is the head of the church, whether bishop, pope, pastor, General Assembly, or congregational committee. Christ is the head of the church, and our whole Constitution is devoted to helping Presbyterians develop a pattern of organization, a dynamic of worship, a structure for discipline, and a set of theological convictions that best enable the Christian community called Presbyterian to discern the mind of Christ for the church and for the world.

My friend and colleague Stated Clerk Bill Chapman has written this wonderful new book, *Finding Christ in the Book of Order.* It gives testimony to the centrality of Christ for our life together as Presbyterians. He focuses on the first four paragraphs (G-1.0100) of the *Book of Order*, which themselves focus on the foundation stone for all that follows in our Constitution—Jesus Christ!

When Jesus asked Peter, "Who do you say that I am?" Peter responded, "You are the Messiah, the Son of the living God." Jesus was emphatic when he replied to this bold affirmation, "On this rock I will build my church, and the gates of hell shall not prevail against it" (Matt. 16:15–16, 18). It is precisely on this rock that Presbyterians have built their Constitution and their church, and Bill Chapman makes this abundantly and persuasively clear in this important new work. He inspires us all with fresh insights into the core Presbyterian conviction that "God has put all things under the Lordship of Jesus Christ and has made Christ Head of the Church, which is his body" (G-1.0100a).

There is a fresh hunger in our time for encountering Christ, both in the church and in the culture at large. We seek Christ through worship, through spiritual disciplines, through the study of Scripture, and through active engagement in the mission of Christ in the world. But all too rarely do we seek to find Christ in our *Book of Order*. But we should! And this new book by Bill Chapman goes a long way in correcting that oversight and in helping us to see what a rich resource our Constitution is for strengthening our walk with Christ.

In the Office of the General Assembly we are launching a major new churchwide project entitled "Common Faith, Common Mission," for which *Finding Christ in the Book of Order* will be an invaluable resource. Our hope is to help all Presbyterians reclaim and unite around the core values of our Presbyterian tradition, which are nowhere better articulated than in the first four chapters of the *Book of Order.* The very starting point of those first four chapters is the main point of *Finding Christ in the Book of Order*—namely, that Jesus Christ is the living head of the church and that Christ gives the church "its faith and life, its unity and mission, its officers and ordinances" (G-1.0100c).

I strongly recommend this book to all Presbyterians—and to all who want to understand the great strength of the Presbyterian tradition that begins with a joyous affirmation of the Lordship of Jesus Christ. It is an excellent book for officer training, for adult study groups, for introducing those coming from other traditions to Presbyterianism, and for private reflection and devotional study.

I urge you to read this provocative and inspirational account of what matters most to Presbyterians and, in so doing, to find Christ anew in the *Book of Order.* You won't be disappointed!

Clifton Kirkpatrick
Stated Clerk
Office of the General Assembly
Presbyterian Church (U.S.A.)

Passages from the
Book of Order

All power in heaven and earth is given to Jesus Christ by
    Almighty God,
        who raised Christ from the dead and set him above
                all rule and authority,
                all power and dominion, and
                every name that is named,
        not only in this age but also in that which is to come.
God has put all things under the Lordship of Jesus Christ
        and has made Christ Head of the Church, which is his body.
                            (G-1.0100a)

Christ calls the Church into being,
giving it all that is necessary
    for its mission to the world,
    for its building up, and
    for its service to God.
Christ is present with the Church in both Spirit and Word.
It belongs to Christ alone
    to rule,
    to teach,
    to call, and
    to use the Church as he wills,
        exercising his authority
        by the ministry of women and men
for the establishment and extension of his Kingdom.
                            (G-1.0100b)

Christ gives to his Church
    its faith and life,
    its unity and mission,
    its officers and ordinances.
Insofar as Christ's will for the Church
    is set forth in Scripture,
    it is to be obeyed.
In the worship and service of God
    and the government of the church,
    matters are to be ordered
    according to the Word
    by reason and sound judgment,
    under the guidance of the Holy Spirit.
                       (G-1.0100c)

In affirming with the earliest Christians that Jesus is Lord,
    the Church confesses that
        he is its hope and
        that the Church, as Christ's body,
    is bound to his authority and
        thus free to live in the lively, joyous reality
    of the grace of God.
                       (G-1.0100d)

Overlook

"Finding Christ" is a phrase that is difficult for me to write or say. Jesus Christ finds us where we are. If such were not the case, we would be in serious trouble. The essence of the Good News is that Jesus Christ finds us, a quest arising from God's amazing love for you and me.

Yet we hunger for more understanding, for the witness of others who share the pilgrimage of faith with us. We read the New Testament, then expand our quest into what others say and write about their faith, their encounters with Christ. It is from other Christian disciples that we learn new aspects of our faith. We come to appreciate what it means to be part of the church that transcends geography, denominations, time itself.

The quest for spiritual food leads each of us into an interesting yet challenging search. There are dead ends, "discoveries" that seem to evaporate when exposed to the difficulties of faithful living. There are also more lasting insights from which we find continuing nourishment consistent with the witness of Scripture. Sometimes these surprise us while we are looking for something else. This book deals with a source for Presbyterians that many seem to have overlooked: the *Book of Order*.

I propose that the four initial paragraphs of G-1.0100 summarize how Presbyterians have demonstrated their commitment to the biblical witness in defining our particular community of faith. They invite us to reflect on how we might energize one another to move forward in the mission to which the Lord of the church has called us. The book's objective is not to propose a specific statement or solution to some current controversy, but to propose a framework for working together from what appear to be axioms or middle terms, those understandings that are the foundation of our polity.

Overlook is an ambiguous word requiring a context in order for its meaning to be clear. When someone says, "I overlooked that possibility," they admit that they ignored or missed something they should have considered. Sometimes what one has overlooked turns out to bring with it serious consequences. A driver who overlooks a traffic sign may get a traffic ticket for careless driving. Persons holding official positions in businesses or organizations are held responsible for what they should have known about practices within their organization.

I "discovered" the first four paragraphs in the *Book of Order* of the Presbyterian Church (U.S.A.) as a polity teacher. I realized that I had overlooked G-1.0100. It was the experience of regularly dealing with seminarians and their questions about polity that gradually led me to an increasing appreciation for these paragraphs. I thank all those seminarians for their probing as well as their insistence that polity required a theological base.

Have these paragraphs been overlooked? The *Annotated Book of Order* is where actions of the General Assembly and its Permanent Judicial Commission are displayed, paragraph by paragraph. There is, as of 2002, only one entry pertaining to G–1.0100, and that is a reference to Overture 00-21 from the Presbytery of Northumberland to the 212th General Assembly (2000). The overture proposed rewriting paragraphs G-1.0100 b, c, and d, inserting references to the role of Scripture. The presbytery, concerned about "the lack of a shared understanding concerning the place and role of Scripture," offered nine "needs" in the life of our denomination that they felt would be met if their proposed revisions were adopted. The General Assembly chose not to approve the overture.[1]

I have pondered, "Why have these paragraphs been overlooked?" One possibility is that we don't expect to find such a compact theological statement in the *Book of Order*. As I argued in my earlier book, *History and Theology in the Book of Order*,[2] there is a tendency for Presbyterians to consider the *Book of Order* more as a manual of operations than as the result of working out the practical implications of our Reformed theology. We tend to focus on the specific question to which we want information when we open the *Book of Order*. Consequently we may consider theological material irrelevant to our concern, something for which we all need to seek forgiveness. I have been struck by the fact that in the recent discussions of the nature of Jesus Christ, particularly on how the church is related to its Lord, that the discussion has thus far been without references to G-1.0100.

A second possibility is that this brief section, "The Head of the Church," comes at the beginning and seems to assert something we assume that we know. We know that the head of the church is Jesus Christ, whose name appears eleven times in this section as "Jesus" or "Jesus Christ," along with seven pronouns referring to Christ. We expect to turn to the *Book of Confessions* when we are exploring our heritage as heirs of the Reformed tradition. One consequence is that many of us miss the connection between the two volumes of our Constitution (G-1.0500), or at least are unclear as to how these pieces fit together. What is sad is that these connections are spelled out for us in what we have overlooked.

A third possibility is that we have neglected to consider the *Book of Order* as a book to be read from the beginning. Whether it is our focus on solving a particular problem, or our hurry when dealing with what at first seems irrelevant, we have failed to give these four paragraphs the attention they deserve. Perhaps there is a tendency to dismiss the *Book of Order* as not worthy of a careful, reflective reading, of engaging the text with our questions and being open to fresh understandings.

Fourth, these paragraphs arose as a part of the reunion process, which was completed in 1983. While there were theological affirmations in both predecessor volumes, the *Book of Order* of the United Presbyterian Church in the United States of America and the *Book of Church Order* of the Presbyterian Church in the United States, the text of these four paragraphs was a result of the reunion process. Further discussion of its origins will be found in the Appendix.

Finally, it is possible that there is a "cloud of witnesses" who have found nourishment for their spiritual life in these four paragraphs, as well as in the text that follows. I applaud them and hope that these reflections may contribute to their deepening appreciation for our Presbyterian heritage. If this book enlarges the number of Presbyterians who are nourished from these paragraphs, I will consider my labors richly blessed.

While *overlook* can mean to omit or ignore, the other meaning of the word is primarily connected to its meaning as a noun: a place from which to view things below. We find overlooks beside highways, proving an opportunity to pull off the road and get a view of the countryside. In some places, these opportunities for a vista are filled with families, many taking pictures of the scene.

I propose that G-1.0100 provides an overlook as one opens the *Book of Order*, an opportunity to see what its purpose is.

On a vacation visit to Texas in August 2001, I learned about oak wilt, a disease affecting certain oak trees. This fungus is fatal to affected trees, with its two-pronged direct attack strategy focusing on the circulatory system of the tree. One pathway of distribution, what is called "the aboveground vector," is through a certain species of beetle attracted by the sap of the tree. The disease can be spread from tree to tree as the beetle seeks food. The other vector is through the interconnected roots of oak trees, an underground approach. Infection by the fungus "clogs the vascular system of oak trees, preventing the flow of nutrients and water."[3]

The fungus can be unwittingly transmitted by human agency. When dead trees are cut down for firewood, distribution of the pieces carries the fungus to new localities. Unless the wood has been dried under plastic for six months prior to distribution, the fungus infects those susceptible varieties of oaks in the vicinity.

What is sobering to those who appreciate having oak trees is that by the time leaf damage symptoms, such as fading color or outer edges turning inward, appear, the tree is probably already fatally infected. While oaks can be inoculated through the use of plugs soaked by the fungicide, the prospects of healing an infected tree are poor.

This illustration from the field of botany struck me with special force since many have become increasingly concerned that we in the Presbyterian Church (U.S.A.) have neglected our roots. Proponents of various perspectives have emerged offering varying diagnoses with varying degrees of appeal. There has been considerable discussion, even some pointed accusations with vigorous responses, without any single perspective mustering a convincing degree of support. Many seem to consider this ferment risky, fearing schism as a consequence.

Since colonial days, Presbyterians have used the phrase "essential tenets" as one way to identify what is basic to our fellowship.[4] We have experimented with various formulations determined by governing bodies at differing levels at different times. This quest has continued for over two and a half centuries. The consequence has been frequent controversy without lasting success. We need to be aware of these attempts at identifying the essential tenets, which will be a part of this study. This review reminds us that the struggle and the accompanying rhetoric perhaps are an uncomfortable reminder that "we have this treasure in clay jars" (2 Cor. 4:7), that we will likely not soon come to some formulation immune to our affirmation that being Reformed includes continuing reformation according to the Word of God and the leading of God's Spirit (see G-2.0200, last sentence).

I am proposing an alternative approach to the *Book of Order*, one rooted in Scripture as well as faithful to our confessions and our Presbyterian process: What if we viewed the *Book of Order* as a developing body of wisdom, something worth careful reflection?

The wisdom books in Scripture have recently received increasing attention as sources of understanding of life and values in biblical times. The sage observed the dilemmas of life, and sought to make sense of them from a faith stance. I suggest that our *Book of Order* is better approached as a record of how the Presbyterian Church (U.S.A.) is dealing with the dilemmas of life in our denomination.

The annual dating and varying colors for each edition of the *Book of Order* remind us that it is a work in progress. This is necessary because of the amendment process we follow, and the numerous proposals for changes that come to the General Assembly each year. Each proposed change comes from some governing body seeking to be the church in a specific situation.

The wisdom sections of Scripture remind readers that our human condition is filled with dilemmas, which are challenges to determine how to be faithful to God in a given time and place. The Bible records instances when emerging challenges were met with choices that were not pleasing to God, and that required later major course changes. Commitment to biblical faithfulness requires awareness that our choices made at a specific time apparently on the basis of our faith later are found to be less adequate than was initially thought. The Old Testament prophets had a major role in reminding God's people of their need to review, and sometimes reconsider, what they felt was the proper course for serving their Lord.

A classic instance of such reconsideration of what constituted the basic faith of Israel is the account of Josiah's reform found in 2 Kings 22–23 and 2 Chronicles 34–35. What amazes the reader is the account of what had become acceptable in the Temple (described in 2 Kings 23:4ff.). Josiah's response to the "discovery" of the Torah scroll[5] is to call for a rededication of the people on the basis of this "new" emergence of Israel's heritage in what began as a renovation of the Temple.

The "confessing church" movement emerged in the Presbyterian Church (U.S.A.) in 2001 as a quest for basic Christian faith and security. Adherents were also troubled by decisions at different levels of the church regarding issues that seemed to them were destroying basic aspects of Christian faith within the Presbyterian Church (U.S.A.). They understood themselves to be utilizing G-9.0102b as the basis for their enterprise: "They [governing bodies] may frame symbols of faith, bear testimony against error in doctrine and immorality in life." The movement appears to overlook the following comment (G-9.0103): "All governing bodies of the church are united by the nature of the church and share with one another responsibilities, rights and powers as provided in this Constitution."

In this book, the text of G-1.0100 is printed in sections at the beginning of each chapter. The format differs from the formal text in the *Book of Order* by breaking the text into units of thought, similar to what is used in blank verse. I hope that this will assist the reader to slow down the pace of reading, enabling an appreciation of the power of G-1.0100. This formatting is a byproduct of my teaching experience of encouraging students to a deeper appreciation of what they were studying.

While these reflections are mine, including such errors and limitations as are part of our human condition, I am deeply appreciative of the many persons who have contributed to making this book possible. Of particular help to me are Elder Clifford Sherrod, who assisted by reading the manuscript and graciously providing corrections and encouragement, and Sandra Sorem and her staff at Witherspoon Press, who have supported this enterprise in the technical ways that are essential and too seldom appreciated. Most of all, I thank my wife, Zitta, who kept me writing by her encouragement, patience, and love, as well as by digging through initial very rough drafts and saving me from many embarrassing gaffes.

Notes:

1. *Minutes of the 212th General Assembly*, volume I, *Journal*, pp. 384–385.

2. William E. Chapman, *History and Theology in the Book of Order: Blood on Every Page* (Louisville, Ky.: Witherspoon Press, 1999).

3. The technical name of the fungus is *Ceratocystis fagacearum*. The beetles are nitidulid beetles. (From "Oak Wilt Disease," on www.oak-wilt.com.)

4. This phrase assumed new prominence when the third ordination question (G-14.0207c and G-14.0405b(3)) was revised in 1967 to include the phrase "essential tenets." This phrase has been a keystone of our Presbyterian tradition since 1758, as indicated in a footnote to G-6.0108b.

5. Generally understood to be a version of what we now call the book of Deuteronomy.

1. *All power in heaven and earth is given to Jesus Christ by*
2. *Almighty God,*
3. *who raised Christ from the dead and set him above*
4. *all rule and authority,*
5. *all power and dominion, and*
6. *every name that is named,*
7. *not only in this age but also in that which is to come.*
8. *God has put all things under the Lordship of Jesus Christ*
9. *and has made Christ Head of the Church, which is his body.*

(G-1.0100a)

1

Beginning

Ask Presbyterians where the two-sentence declaration on page 20 comes from, and the response will most likely be "the Bible." Other, more literate Presbyterians might refer to the *Book of Confessions* but would not be able to identify which confession is the source. Most would be astonished to learn that it comes from the *Book of Order*.

Presbyterians usually expect rules of one sort or another when they turn to the *Book of Order*. Just as one expects recipes in a cookbook, or definitions in a dictionary, many Presbyterians turn to this book to see whether there is a rule or prohibition that would limit what they would like to do. Such expectation carries with it a notion that there would be no benefit from reading the *Book of Order* as a book, since it is considered to be a technical reference manual. Who would begin reading the dictionary at the beginning? The purpose seems to be to look things up, not to read the text through.

I intend by these reflections to share my discovery, made while introducing seminarians to the rich treasures in the *Book of Order*, that there are jewels of theological insight scattered throughout its text. These jewels are not substitutes for Scripture, but they provide distillations of scriptural truth worthy of careful attention. I have found that the beauty and felicity of many of these passages surprise, bless, and then challenge me to stretch into what Paul called "the measure of the full stature of Christ" (Eph. 4:13).

Given these expectations, the opening sentences startle a reader like a sudden light on a dark day. Expecting "business as usual" as we enter the second of the two Presbyterian Constitutional books,[1] we find ourselves transported to a realm beyond our imagining, into that most intimate of relationships, between two persons of the Trinity. In one sentence, we find a rephrasing of Philippians 2:5–11, often called the oldest Christian hymn. We find ourselves in a time before time, awed not only that we are glimpsing eternity, but also by the mystery that is the basis for our faith. The opening sentence hits us with the force of Moses' burning bush experience (Exodus 3) and the intensity of Isaiah's experience in the Temple amid a national crisis (Isaiah 6). We find ourselves in that time when "all things came into being through [the Word]."[2]

Such affirmations push us to our knees. We have been thrust into the heart of Holiness itself. The Old Testament depicts what scholars call "Yahweh's council," most notably in 1 Kings 22:19–23 and Isaiah 6.[3] Both of these scenes come to prophets who are awed by what they see. It is into just this divine council of the Triune God that G-1.0100a invites us, when we are willing to pause to soak in the vision. The *Book of Order* begins with nothing less than the glory of the Lord! Walter Brueggemann's discussion of the implications of 1 Kings 22:19–23 culminates with the comment, "Thus 'divine council' is a strategem for linking Yahweh and the human enterprise, Yahweh and the prophetic assertion."[4]

Of course, there is more to the story. A morning prayer for use during Advent begins, "Holy God, the mystery of your eternal Word took flesh among us in Jesus Christ."[5] It is striking that this major document of our denomination begins just as Luke begins his account of the advent of Christ among us, with the "glory of the Lord." That simple phrase also echoes the Psalms, where it occurs in thirty-six psalms. Prophets, notably Isaiah and Ezekiel, repeat this simple, yet profound, way of praising God's splendor. The Latin phrase *mysterium tremendum et fascinans*,[6] popularized by Rudolf Otto in his book *The Idea of the Holy*, offers another way of alluding to God's greatness. We are invited, as we enter the *Book of Order*, to "worship the Lord in holy splendor" (Ps. 96:9). To pass by or ignore such an opening reminder of what we are about as disciples of the Good News of Jesus Christ is to risk forgetting that we are called to be faithful in our life together.

Appreciating the glory of the Trinity as well as the glory the shepherds saw gives greater understanding of the ancient Christian hymn Paul cites:

> Let the same mind be in you that was in Christ Jesus,
> who, though he was in the form of God,
>> did not count equality with God
>> as something to be exploited,
> but emptied himself,
>> taking the form of a slave,
>> being born in human likeness. (Phil. 2:5–7)

Never has there been a renunciation like this! From co-creator to human being— willingly, even to the point of radical humiliation and death as a criminal.

The hymn doesn't end there, just as the gospel of Jesus goes beyond the apparent end—the Resurrection. As the Philippians hymn puts it:

> Therefore God also highly exalted him
>> and gave him the name
>> that is above every name,
> so that at the name of Jesus
>> every knee should bend,
>> in heaven and on earth and under the earth,
> and every tongue should confess
>> that Jesus Christ is Lord,
>> to the glory of God the Father. (Phil. 2:9–11)

Jesus' resurrection from the dead and ascension into heaven are the testimonies to this affirmation of Jesus as Lord. How simple the affirmation, that Jesus Christ is Lord! The words come almost automatically, without the briefest consideration of what we are confessing! We use the title "Lord Jesus" without reflecting that this attributes to the risen Jesus all the power and status outlined in this first sentence of the *Book of Order*.

The first sentence opens on holy ground, where our best words fail to express what is in our hearts and souls. We are ushered into God's holy presence, something beyond words yet needing to be shared, using words of praise as faulty tools to clothe our thanksgiving. We react in various ways—singing, praising, bowing, raising hands, kneeling, or simply remaining silent—realizing that there is no adequate way of expressing God's presence. We are brought up short in our quest for "how to" as we encounter God who is.

Not only is there awe at the outset of the *Book of Order*, as we have noted. There is also an awesome scope in this sentence evident in the word *all* repeated three times, followed by the synonym *every*. The repetition emphasizes the immensity of scope appropriate for describing the One who is Lord.

The statement opens with "*all* power and authority" (emphasis added). Consider what *power* means. Walter Wink has written extensively and helpfully about power, yet begins his exploration by writing, "The reader of this work will search in vain for a definition of power."[7] While noting that "the language of power pervades the New Testament,"[8] Wink also found in his exegetical work that "the language of power in the New Testament is imprecise, liquid, interchangeable, and unsystematic."[9] While patterns of usage were evident, Wink contends that "because these terms are interchangeable, one or a pair or a series can be made to represent them all."[10] This suggests that by using pairs of terms, the *Book of Order* is consistent with Scripture in pairing terms which might appear to us redundant, yet witness to the scope of the affirmation. In short, *all* in this passage means ALL in the most comprehensive sense possible.

Wink suggests that the most comprehensive presentation of the scope of "powers" is found in Colossians 1:16:[11]

> . . . for in him ["our Lord Jesus Christ"] all things in heaven and on earth were created, things visible and invisible, whether thrones or dominions or rulers or powers—all things have been created through him and for him.

Compared with this passage, G-1.0100a seems understated. At the same time, the inclusiveness of the lordship of Jesus Christ certainly extends beyond what is usually called the spiritual realm.

The shift from "all" to "every" maintains the emphasis on comprehensiveness, while also expanding the reference now to "every name that is named." Such a phrase suggests that the linguistic chaos since the Tower of Babel (Gen. 11:1–9) is subject now to the lordship of Jesus Christ. "Every name" of every person who has ever held some form of power throughout human history (line 6)! We have yet another comprehensive assertion, which upon reflection takes our breath away by its scope and implication.

After reading Psalm 2, where God gives to his Son "the nations for your inheritance," the editors of *Daily Prayer* insert this prayer as meditation on the affirmation of God's rule:

> Sovereign God,
> you gave us your only begotten to be the Savior of the world,
> and you crowned him with grace to rule over all.
> Give us humility
> that we might faithfully serve him
> and so know the joy
> given to all who take refuge in Christ our Lord. Amen.[12]

We find the final adjective "all" in G-1.0100a in the second sentence (line 7), concluding the paean of praise with the simple recognition of Christ's lordship over *all* things. We now acknowledge that we are not simply referring to "all things" in the Presbyterian Church (U.S.A.), or "all things" Christian or spiritual, but to "all things," all creation.

A similar affirmation is found in the Second Helvetic Confession:

> There is, indeed, another power that is pure and absolute, which is called the power of right. According to this power all things in the whole world are subject to Christ, who is Lord of all, as he himself has testified when he said: "All authority in heaven and on earth has been given to me" (Matt. 28:18), and again, "I am the first and the last, and behold I am alive for evermore, and I have the keys of Hades and Death" (Rev. 1:18); also, "He has the key of David, which opens and no one shall shut, who shuts and no one opens" (Rev. 3:7).[13]

The tone of this confession resonates with line 7 of G-1.0100a. Such a quotation begins to show consistency between the two volumes of the Presbyterian Constitution.

To affirm that Jesus is Lord is to recognize that "all things" in its most comprehensive sense belong first of all to Jesus our Savior and Lord. When we make this confession of faith, we assume the new identity of stewards of all that belongs to God, which is not less than everything. It is an all-or-nothing affirmation.

There is only one line left, the second part of a double predicate (line 8). It is with this final comment that the ineffable faith in the Trinity leads us into more familiar territory of the church. We are moving toward more familiar language, yet with a difference.

One of the major contributions of the Westminster Confession of Faith was the distinction between the visible and the invisible church. The first paragraph in the chapter "Of the Church" is a slightly more expanded description than is given in line 8 of G-1.0100a.

The catholic or universal church, which is invisible, consists of the whole number of the elect, that have been, are, or shall be gathered into one, under Christ the head thereof; and is the spouse, the body, the fullness of Him that filleth all in all. (C-6.140)

The catholic, or universal, and invisible church includes "the whole number of the elect, that have been, are, or shall be gathered into one." This goes way beyond ecumenical concern. It is the church in this sense to which all people are drawn by God's grace and love.

The Westminster Confession continues, describing another form of church:

The visible Church, which is also catholic or universal under the gospel (not confined to one nation as before under the law), consists of all those throughout the world that profess the true religion, together with their children; and is the Kingdom of the Lord Jesus Christ; the house and family of God, through which men are ordinarily saved and union with which is essential to their best growth and service. (C-6.141)

The visible church is the one we know about, the one we can see. It is comprised of those who profess faith, together with their children; it is "the house and family of God, through which [people] are ordinarily saved." Note also that growth and service are fostered for those who unite with the visible church.

The consequences of these differences, first positive and then negative, are spelled out in the Confession as follows:

This catholic Church hath been sometimes more, sometimes less, visible. And particular churches, which are members thereof, are more or less pure, according as the doctrine of the gospel is taught and embraced, ordinances administered, and public worship performed more or less purely in them. (C-6.143)

The purest churches under heaven are subject both to mixture and error: and some have so degenerated as to become apparently no churches of Christ. Nevertheless, there shall be always a Church on earth, to worship God according to his will. (C-6.144)

While the visible church has a positive mission implementing the mission given to it by its Lord, the visible church is always a "mixed crowd," a phrase that appears in Exodus 12:38 describing the people who made up the exodus.

The determination of how much mixture and of what sort has been a dilemma for church people since at least the fourth century, when the Council of Rome confirmed the decision of a synod meeting in Carthage to permit those who had previously denied their faith during persecution to be restored. In North Africa, a priest named Donatus opposed the naming of a bishop of Carthage who was considered a renouncer, took over the diocese, and began a movement to "purify" the church. Although his followers, called Donatists, were denounced by the church and the theologian Augustine of Hippo, the movement continued into the middle of the fifth century. Many contend that Augustine's major work, *The City of God*, was at least partially an attack on the Donatists who were seeking the purification of the church.

The Westminster Divines contended that there was no possibility of the faithful making the church pure. There will always be, as one seminary professor often remarked, "the Old Adam in the New Jerusalem."[14] Such a pronouncement may seem to doom the church to ineffectual and tragic attempts at ministry. However, it serves as a reminder that discipleship is always a paradoxical experience, that we have "this treasure in clay jars" (2 Cor. 4:7).

To balance this reminder of the fragility of the church, this paragraph from the Westminster Confession continues with a hopeful "nevertheless." The assurance, the promise, is a bold statement that "there shall be *always* a Church on earth, to worship God according to his will" [emphasis added]. Today we might say, "appearances to the contrary notwithstanding." The *Book of Order* catches this hint of hope when we find the assertion that "The Church of Jesus Christ is the provisional demonstration of what God intends for all humanity" (G-3.0200). Our church is certainly not pure, yet it presses on "toward the goal for the prize of the heavenly call of God in Christ Jesus" (Phil. 3:14).

William Placher, in his book *The Domestication of Transcendence: How Modern Thinking about God Went Wrong*,[15] contends that

> Christians have always, in one degree or another, failed to notice God's initiatives toward the world, sought to move God under their own power, and thereby fallen into idolatry. But certain ways of doing so became more pervasive, I believe, in the seventeenth century, as an earlier sense of the divine mystery, the wonder of grace, and the inadequacy of human talk about God tended to get lost.[16]

Drawing on the discussions of Thomas Aquinas, Martin Luther, and John Calvin, whom he considers a "control group" for subsequent theological discussions of God's transcendence,[17] Placher conducts his careful analysis of our situation. Commenting on the English Puritans, some of whom participated in the Westminster Assembly, he comments:

> The Puritans would in principle have agreed with Calvin that salvation comes through grace alone and on the importance of Christian freedom, but, looking within themselves for assurance that they had received it, many of them became concerned about their works. In times of social disorder, some of them worried about the destabilizing effects of utterly unpredictable grace.[18]

The paradox of God's grace, the essence of the Good News, becomes a challenge to faithfulness in our modern age where predictability is often considered the hallmark of order. Placher reminds us that God's order for the world as for the church, not to mention our lives, is the order of adventure, of trusting confidence to take yet another step, always trusting that God's transcendent love will sustain us.

The second aspect of God's design in the final sentence of G-1.0100a reminds us that Christ is head of the church. This assertion again reflects the twenty-fifth chapter of the Westminster Confession, this time recalling the final section of that chapter:

> The Lord Jesus Christ is the only head of the Church, and the claim of any man [*sic*] to be the vicar of Christ and the head of the Church, is without warrant in fact or in Scripture, even anti-Christian, a usurpation dishonoring to the Lord Jesus Christ. (C-6.145)

For those in the Westminster Assembly, this was a defining remark, separating them from both the Roman Catholic Church, which understood the pope to be the vicar of Christ on earth, and hence the head of that church, on the one hand, and the Anglican Church on the other hand, which understood the English monarch to be the head of that church. To assert that the only head of the church is Jesus Christ was to differentiate them from these other understandings, a courageous stand in the light of the recent controversy between King Charles I and Parliament over this precise point.[19]

Today we Americans see such a statement as an early indication of what our Constitution enshrined as the principle of separation of church and state through the First Amendment. In the *Book of Confessions*, we Presbyterians have included the Theological Declaration of Barmen, which demonstrates how significant this understanding is when a people is confronted with a totalitarian view of all social institutions. Two paragraphs from that document remind us of how relevant it is to maintain such an understanding:

> The Church's commission, upon which its freedom is founded, consists in delivering the message of the free grace of God to all people in Christ's stead, and therefore in the ministry of his own Word and work through sermon and sacrament.
> We reject the false doctrine, as though the Church in human arrogance could place the Word and work of the Lord in the service of any arbitrarily chosen desires, purposes, and plans. (C-8.26–.27)

There is a defiant tone of courage here that energizes us.

There is also the warning that is as important today as it was in the mid-twentieth century, against "any arbitrarily chosen desires, purposes, and plans." The standard is what the head of the church, Jesus Christ, calls us to do, not what someone understands as a consequence of what Christ taught. This is a delicate, difficult distinction, to be approached with utmost care. Perhaps we need to recall the biblical and confessional admonition that ministers are "stewards of the mysteries of God,"[20] not as things to be solved, but as recognizing that our understanding of what Christ wants of the church ought never to be confused with what Christ's agenda is in reality. A century before the Westminster Confession, Heinrich Bullinger, in the Second Helvetic Confession, suggested how ministers were to be considered:

> Therefore, the apostle wants us to think of ministers as ministers.[21] Now the apostle calls them υπηρετας, rowers, who have their eyes fixed on the coxswain, and so men who do not live for themselves or according to their own will, but for others—namely, their masters, upon whose command they altogether depend. For in all his duties every minister of the Church is commanded to carry out only what he has received in commandment from his Lord, and not to indulge his own free choice. And in this case it is expressly declared who is the Lord, namely, Christ; to whom the ministers are subject in all the affairs of the ministry. (C-5.155)

This is not an easy way to proceed in ministry, but it is essential for the health of the church that this be the intent and goal of those who serve as officers in the church.

The Presbyterians I know seldom refer to the church as "the body of Christ." Perhaps that is due to Presbyterian understanding of humility. Perhaps it is because so many of us are so keenly aware of the trials and weaknesses of our churches as we seek to go about serving our Lord. Perhaps it is because there is a sense that "the Body of Christ" is just too holy. For whatever reason, the *Book of Order* reminds us at the end of G-1.0100a that our church, as it is, is still the body of Christ.

The metaphor is certainly biblical (see Col. 1:18; Rom. 12:4–5; Eph. 4:4–16; and 1 Cor. 12, which is its most extensive delineation). There are at least two possible ways to understand the apostle Paul's metaphor. One is theological, as a consequence of the resurrection of Jesus Christ. Throughout the centuries the debate over where the body of Christ is has been focused on the implications for the way Christians understand the Lord's Supper. If Christ be ascended into heaven, as we affirm in the Apostles' Creed, how then can Christ be present to the church as it gathers around the Lord's Table? Certainly, Paul records as Jesus' explicit teaching his saying to his disciples, on his last night on earth, "This is my body broken for you," as he fed them in the upper room.[22]

The Heidelberg Catechism responds to the question with four questions and answers relating to Communion. Question 79 and its response suggest an answer from our *Book of Confessions*:

> **Q. 79.** Then why does Christ call the bread his body, and the cup his blood, or the New Covenant in his blood, and why does the apostle Paul call the Supper "a means of sharing" in the body and blood of Christ?

A. Christ does not speak in this way except for a strong reason. He wishes to teach us by it that as bread and wine sustain this temporal life so his crucified body and shed blood are the true food and drink of our souls for eternal life. Even more, he wishes to assure us by this visible sign and pledge that we come to share in his true body and blood through the working of the Holy Spirit as surely as we receive with our mouth these holy tokens in remembrance of him, and that all his sufferings and his death are our own as certainly as if we had ourselves suffered and rendered satisfaction in our own persons. (C-4.079)

The "strong reason" for such language is to remind us of how Jesus' dying on the cross is the source of sustenance for our discipleship. The focus here is on how each of us is nourished spiritually for obedience to our Savior and Lord.

The same Jesus inspires Paul to tell the Corinthians, hardly paragons of virtue or understanding or love: "*You* are the body of Christ and individually members of it" (emphasis added) (1 Cor. 12:27). The context makes it evident that the metaphor of the body relates to how Christ can be both the ascended Lord of all and at work on the earth among those who had treated him so poorly. This connects us with the church of which you and I are members, those of us seeking to be faithful disciples. There is a physicality in this second sense that confronts us with an uncomfortable realization: that Jesus Christ expects those who profess to be part of his body to function according to his purpose, to be obedient to his will. Part of this is also a recognition that not every member has the same function. The emphasis is that the head of the body, Jesus Christ, is the one who directs the actions of the members so that Christ's purpose is moved forward.

Mission becomes obedient action, as does everything else the church is doing. We live at a time when physical fitness to some degree or another is understood as a key to health and longer life. When we are "out of shape," we don't function as well as we would like to. Just so with the church. The *Book of Order* describes the church's role as the body of Christ in this way: "The Church of Jesus Christ is the provisional demonstration of what God intends for all humanity" (G-3.0200). Following this sobering, awesome declaration there are three short paragraphs outlining how we as Presbyterians understand the implications of being the body of Christ. The theme is the "new reality" brought to us by Jesus Christ. What is tragic is how seldom these calls to mission and witness are studied, much less heeded.

The first paragraph of the *Book of Order* moves from the mysterious and unknowable depth of eternity at the moment of Creation to our present responsibility to serve our Savior with faith and love. By any criterion, such an accomplishment is worthy of our thankfulness for such a concise, direct, readily understandable introduction to who we are as Presbyterians and what we seek to accomplish. How surprising that we pay so little attention to this powerful challenge to be about our appropriate work.

Notes

1. G-1.0500 reads as follows: "The *Constitution of the Presbyterian Church (U.S.A.)* consists of *The Book of Confessions* and the *Book of Order*."

2. John 1:3, using the noun rather than the pronoun.

3. See Walter Brueggemann, *Theology of the Old Testament* (Minneapolis: Fortress Press, 1997). Brueggemann's discussion begins on p. 628.

4. Ibid., p. 629.

5. *Daily Prayer: The Worship of God,* Supplemental Liturgical Resource 5, prepared by the Office of Worship for the Presbyterian Church (U.S.A.) and the Cumberland Presbyterian Church (Philadelphia: Westminster Press, 1987), p. 104.

6. "A tremendous and fascinating mystery."

7. Walter Wink, *Naming the Powers: The Language of Power in the New Testament* (Philadelphia: Fortress Press, 1984), p. 3. The other books in his series The Powers are *Unmasking the Powers: The Invisible Forces That Determine Human Existence* (1986), and *Engaging the Powers: Discernment and Resistance in a World of Domination* (1992).

8. Ibid., p. 7.

9. Ibid., p. 9.

10. Ibid., p. 10.

11. Ibid., p. 11.

12. *Daily Prayer,* p. 183.

13. *Book of Confessions*, 5.157. Note that the context for this passage has to do with "The Power of Ministers of the Church." Subsequent references to the *Book of Confessions* are prefaced by C-.

14. Norman Victor Hope made this remark when he taught church history at Princeton Theological Seminary.

15. William Placher, *The Domestication of Transcendence: How Modern Thinking about God Went Wrong* (Louisville, Ky.: Westminster John Knox Press, 1996).

16. Ibid., p. 17.

17. Ibid., p. 3.

18. Ibid., p. 99.

19. "For eleven years, he [Charles I] ruled in church and state after the manner of an oriental despot; that is, without a parliament of reference to the will of the people." Jacob Harris Patton, *A Popular History of the Presbyterian Church in the United States of America* (New York: D. Appleton and Co., 1903), p. 59.

20. Ephesians 3 and C-5.156.

21. "Ministers as ministers" sounds tautological to us. In the previous paragraph Bullinger commented on his understanding of *priest* as a title belonging only to Jesus Christ. In this phrase, he is continuing to clarify how he understands *minister* as a New Testament term. For Presbyterians, "minister" in some places in the Second Helvetic Confession would include functions we assign to elders.

22. 1 Cor. 11:24 KJV. Note that some modern versions omit the word "broken."

1. *Christ calls the Church into being,*
2. *giving it all that is necessary*
3.   *for its mission to the world,*
4.   *for its building up, and*
5.   *for its service to God.*
6. *Christ is present with the Church in both Spirit and Word.*
7. *It belongs to Christ alone*
8.   *to rule,*
9.   *to teach,*
10.   *to call, and*
11.   *to use the Church as he wills,*
12.   *exercising his authority*
13.   *by the ministry of women and men*
14. *for the establishment and extension of his Kingdom.*

(G-1.0100b)

2
Endowment

In the Presbytery of the Palisades, a group of pastors have formed a group to discuss the issues they encounter in their churches, which are partially supported from endowment funds. One issue was, how does a church proceed with stewardship programs when the members know that some part of the operation is already "taken care of"? There was plenty for them to discuss.

How does a church with an endowment encourage members to be faithful in their own stewardship? When there continues to be income from "nonliving sources," as some refer to what comes from invested funds, members readily get into the habit of thinking that what they contribute from their own income will not "make any real difference" in how the church goes about its regular work. Such a predictable response signals the beginning of a decline in the vitality of that church.[1]

A pastor, on learning that the church he was serving was about to receive a bequest in the range of a million dollars, and aware of the danger it presented, proposed to the session that the income from the fund would be dedicated to "special mission projects." That session chose to accept the bequest with that condition, resisting the temptation to use the income for purposes closer to home. Consequently, the church enabled many schools, hospitals, and churches around the world to benefit from the blessing to one church by one of its members.

In an article titled "A Theology of Grace," James Hudnut-Beumler suggests the category of "commonwealth" as a reminder that "[the corpus of an endowment] is wealth and yet . . . the beneficiary of the wealth is not a private individual, but a community."[2] While Hudnut-Beumler's suggestion is certainly helpful and correct as far as it goes, "commonwealth" is not a familiar concept to most citizens of the United States, nor is it rooted explicitly in the Presbyterian understanding of our faith.

Hudnut-Beumler emphasizes the concept of grace by describing endowments as "more like an honor placed upon a boy by a dying father. The boy hopes to be worthy of what he has already been given."[3] The point derived from this is that "endowments should be [seen as] a reminder of blessing, and as permission to live faithfully and graciously."

This comment provides a springboard for considering the text of G-1.0100b, where we find a different endowment for the church, one that is less recognized and appreciated than most other endowments, yet is the most significant and surprising endowment imaginable. After reviewing how the persons of the Trinity cooperated in the creation of the universe, we are now directed to the creation of a people called to follow God's intent for life. "Church" is shorthand for the human community of God's servants throughout history.[4] The Old Testament narrative of how the community of God's people struggled with trusting God becomes our story as well.

One professor suggests that contemporary churches suffer from the disease of "manna indigestion."[5] Such a diagnosis draws on the account in Exodus 16, where God promises to provide Moses and the band of exiles daily bread from heaven. God's gifts are to be used as God intends. The condition for the gift is obedience to two instructions: collect only enough each day for that day, and gather a double portion before the Sabbath.

Like children, the Israelites immediately tested these limitations. Right away, some were collecting more than a daily ration, fearing they would not have enough if the giving stopped. The result was that the next day, the remaining food went bad, "it bred worms and became foul" (Exod. 16:20). The next surprise was that when the double Sabbath portion was saved overnight, there was no spoilage—until the third day, if anyone tried to save it. God's promises and instructions were to be taken seriously and obeyed.

We call this strange heavenly bread *manna*. The Hebrew word actually means "What is it?"—the immediate reaction of those startled wanderers. The naming reinforces the oddness of God's "bread from heaven," something never seen before by the wandering children of Israel. God provided for God's people in a fresh way, then made other provisions for feeding the multitude. God took care of this group who were becoming God's people. The incident reinforces God's introduction to the giving of the Ten Commandments at Mount Sinai. This begins with a reminder that their liberation from slavery under the Egyptians was evidence of God's caring. Obedience to the commandments is based on what has recently taken place. God is the One who provides.

The manna passage is more likely to be used in worship as a metaphor for Communion than for stewardship. Yet it is both. I propose that the stewardship implication is even more powerful, since it resonates with our frequent praying, "Give us this day our daily bread." The *Anchor Bible* commentary on Matthew suggests as the translation of this phrase, "Give us today the bread we need."[6]

Manna may also be considered as a metaphor for God's grace. Gathering and eating manna day by day strikes us as miraculous or amazing. What a wonderful life! We overlook the discipline that comes with manna/grace. This account precedes the subsequent gift of the Ten Commandments, a more familiar incident, yet too seldom seen as another indication of how we are to respond to God's gracious deliverance.

Every breath we take is evidence of God's grace to us. So often we happen to see or hear just the appropriate word, meet the right person, or find that doors open to new adventures, new understandings, new blessings for which we give God humble thanks. We wonder, like those pilgrims in the desert, what we should call it. Often we think it "nice" or "lucky," or even say, "It's about time!" God's grace usually comes to us as surprise.

The Christian life, the existence of the church, continues to be a manna existence. Endowments seem to add permanence, give reassurance. But when the markets convulse, when we find that we have confused power with some ephemeral economic bubble, when there is no longer any security in what we honestly thought was foundational and lasting, the jolt reminds us that our security is in the name of the Lord, the grace of our Lord Jesus Christ, that living faithfully and lovingly gets us through the tough times. The timing of blessings, as well as the determination of which blessing, is up to God the Giver. Eventually we learn that God's manna just keeps coming—usually as surprises, initially unnamed, and finally understood.

Psalm 50 was written to people of an earlier age, when demonstrating their faith was considered to require animal sacrifice. This concern usually reminds us of Micah 6:6–8, culminating in the affirmation that, rather than animal sacrifice, God requires faithful people to "do justice, and to love kindness, and to walk humbly with your God." But Psalm 50 is even more direct where God reminds the faithful that "every wild animal of the forest is mine, the cattle on a thousand hills" (v. 10), so more animals are not appropriate. Rather, the instruction comes, "Offer to God a sacrifice of thanksgiving, and pay your vows to the Most High."

A prayer that reminds us of what it means to praise Jesus as our Lord in a blending of modern terminology yet with evident roots in Scripture is the one that follows the 45th Psalm in the *Book of Common Worship—Daily Prayer*:

> God of majesty,
> you exalted Jesus, the Anointed One,
> that every knee on earth might bow before him.
> Strengthen us to confess him as our Sovereign,
> and to serve him with joy,
> that we might be led even to the marriage supper of the Lamb,
> Christ Jesus our Lord. Amen.[7]

The second phrase of G-1.0100b, "giving it [the church] all that is necessary," reminds us of how God provided for our spiritual ancestors in the desert, as well as how our Savior taught us to pray, "Give us this day . . ." We are reminded of our dependence on God for life itself, for grace that renews and refreshes us, and for the other gifts for which we are too seldom thankful.

The challenge of living by grace is evident in the conversation between Jesus and those who had followed him across the lake (John 6:25–32). The dialogue turns on a misunder-standing of both miracles of feeding multitudes. Jesus reminds his questioners that it wasn't Moses who produced the manna, although they were now asserting that as fact. Jesus was talking about where he had come from in terms of where the manna had come from. Until his hearers were clear on that, they would never comprehend what Jesus was saying. Understanding was also a gift from God.

These biblical incidents remind us that stewardship is fundamentally a challenge of trust. In a world where trust is generally considered an indication of foolishness or gullibility, Christ's call to trust God is no easier than it was for those exiles from Egypt or the recently fed crowd trying to figure out what was going on. "What is it?" continues to be the wondering lament of those who seek to live faithfully.

This reflection on God's historic presence and power enhances our understanding of the verb *gives* in the present tense. God persists in giving, from creation to the fulfillment of God's intention. Expressed theologically, this testifies to the consistency of God's grace.

Many of us are startled by the assertion in G-1.0100b that God gives to the church "*all* that is necessary." This suggests that the church as the community of all the faithful in every time and place has an endowment that for all time will provide whatever is necessary for God's Word to go forth. *Every* church is an endowed church!

"All that is necessary" appears seven times in the *Book of Confessions.* The intent of this phrase is vividly expressed in a question and answer from the Heidelberg Catechism:

Q. 118. What has God commanded us to ask of him?

A. All things *necessary* for soul and body which Christ the Lord has included in the prayer which he himself taught us. (C-4.118)[8]

The reference of the phrase here is personal rather than corporate, where each of us needs to consider what is necessary for our life.

We seldom reflect on what is necessary for our lives as persons. If we ask people what they consider to be the necessities of life, the responses may astound us. There is major diversity in our time. Is a cell phone a necessity or a convenience? Is a car necessary? A television set? A computer? An Internet connection?

Reflecting on what is necessary is difficult, particularly when we encounter those for whom getting life's bare necessities is a daily ordeal. Jesus' parable in Matthew 25:31–46 reminds us that hunger, thirst, estrangement, nakedness, sickness, and incarceration are evidences of being denied what is necessary for life. When some of the items from the previous paragraph are put against Jesus' parable, what is the result?

The phrase presses us to ask, "What *is* necessary for the church's life?" How does the church know whether it is fulfilling the intent of God the Donor of the endowment? Three clauses beginning with the preposition "for" (lines 8–11) suggest an understanding of "necessary." Each of these uses language from the New Testament.

The first of the three clauses is, "for its mission to the world." "Mission" is a word Presbyterians use frequently, yet seldom carefully. We tend to say the word without considering its richness as well as its challenge. The result is misunderstanding, especially when what we say produces results we didn't think we meant, or that are challenged by others whose understanding differs from ours.

How much better it would be if we sat together and worked our way through chapter 3 of the *Book of Order*, titled "The Church and Its Mission." This chapter moves from the witness of Scripture and the doctrine of the Trinity to the scope of mission as we Presbyterians understand it, ending with how we are to engage in mission.

The church's calling, according to G-3.0300, is threefold.

"To tell the good news of salvation" (G-3.0300a) is what many understand as the church's mission to the world. This familiar sense is defined as occurring "in Word and Sacrament." The content of the proclamation is that "the new age has dawned," as well as that "God who creates life, frees those in bondage, forgives sin, reconciles brokenness, makes all things new, is still at work in the world" (G-3.0300a(2)).

"To present the claims of Jesus Christ" (G-3.0300b) leads to a more frequently used definition: "leading persons to repentance, acceptance of him as Savior and Lord, and new life as his disciples." This is what G-1.0100b calls "building up."

"To be Christ's faithful evangelist" (G-3.0300c) is more complex, setting forth how contemporary Presbyterians understand the implications of biblical faith for the scope of mission as "participating in God's activity in the world through its life for others." Mission is thus energized as cooperating with what God is already doing around us. The specifications are breathtaking, each one beginning with a present participle expressing mission as a dynamic. The church participates in God's activity by

healing and reconciling and binding up wounds,
ministering to the needs of the poor, the sick, the lonely,
    and the powerless,
engaging in the struggle to free people from sin, fear,
    oppression, hunger, and injustice,
giving itself and its substance to the service of those who suffer,
sharing with Christ in the establishing of his just, peaceable, and loving
    rule in the world. (G-3.0300c(3)).

It is unfortunate, if not tragic, that so many earnest Presbyterians have ignored the scope of this mission manifesto, preferring to redraft "more focused" statements designed to appeal to specific constituencies.

This description follows a reminder in the chapter (G-3.0200) that the church is the body of Christ, "the provisional demonstration of what God intends for all humanity." Paul's metaphor, found in various forms in the New Testament (Rom. 12:3–8; 1 Cor. 12:12–30; Eph. 4:4–16), emphasizes both the unity of the body as well as its functional diversity. There are many forms mission may take; this requires that those of us who are engaged in mission do the part we are called to perform as best we can, understanding that our sister and brother believers are also doing their utmost, using the gifts they have been given. All to the glory and praise of the One who is Lord of the church.

A second purpose of the endowment comes in line 4, "for its building up." The phrase sends us to 1 Corinthians 3, where the apostle Paul discusses the church as God's building. Paul exhorts the quarreling Corinthians to be "skilled master builders" as they work on their community of faith, always mindful that there is one foundation, Jesus Christ.

The *Book of Confessions* and the *Book of Order* may be understood as the set of plans we Presbyterians have chosen for the design of our part of Christ's kingdom. The plans may need to be revised; architects and engineers sometimes discover that their initial work exposes inadequacies in their blueprints. What we are building is to the glory of God, so the changes we think would improve the building need to be carefully evaluated before they are implemented.

We need reminding that "building up" has significance as well as "mission." There is an active sense in "building up" which we sometimes forget, but which is an ongoing necessity. As cathedrals take years to complete, the "building up" of the Presbyterian Church continues as a priority for all of us. This line also points out that the activity is "building," not simply "maintaining." Business as usual is never an option for those obeying the directive to build.

The historic commitment of Presbyterians to education is one facet of such building. Education is more than publishing or choosing a curriculum to follow, although this is often the impression that comes from observing our discussions. Education is encouraging "growth in grace," which happens in many ways.

Line 5 points to the third purpose for the endowment: "its service to God." We usually use "service" to refer to how we are treated as customers. We complain when we don't get "good service." We may leave a smaller tip in a restaurant, realizing that the original meaning, "to improve prompt service," no longer applies.

There is a biblical use of the word *service* which is different. Romans 12:1 comes to mind: "I appeal to you therefore, brothers and sisters, by the mercies of God, to present your bodies as a living sacrifice, holy and acceptable to God, which is your spiritual service" [NRSV: worship]. The New Revised Standard Version in a footnote offers *reasonable* for *spiritual*. The Greek word is the basis for our word "logical."

The Greek root for *service* is $\lambda\alpha\tau\rho\epsilon\iota\alpha$. Hermann Strathmann's discussion of this term in the *Theological Dictionary of the New Testament* suggests that the word is rooted in Deuteronomy 10:12–13, where the people of Israel are instructed that God requires them to "serve the LORD your God with all your heart and with all your soul." Professor Strathmann comments, "The concrete idea of sacrifice seems always to cling to the noun no less than the verb."[9]

The church's service is that expression of gratitude which energizes praise and prayer, then overflows into the disciplined life of faith where we can become more and more Christlike in our dealings with one another and with our neighbors on this planet.

Following this order, the next sentence (line 6) assures us that Christ is present to the church, and it tells us how Christ is present. The assurance of the presence of Christ is consistent with our confessions, as well as the witness of Scripture. Less agreement surrounds the question of how Christ is present. In this paragraph it is simply that "both Spirit and Word" are the ways by which Christ is present. We will find in the next chapter a more nuanced treatment of Christ's presence. For now we have the tension between "Word" (in the sense of Scripture) and "Spirit," which is more dynamic and less susceptible to precision. The tension is a reminder that the tendency to favor one or the other produces results inconsistent with the witness of our faith. We worship neither the words of Scripture nor the breath of the Spirit that quickens us, but the Lord who is present in both ways. Such a dynamic tension lies at the core of our Presbyterian witness.

Such an assertion emerges from the post-Easter understanding that Jesus Christ was truly human and truly divine. The Lordship of Christ as an expression of faith means that it is the reality of Christ as we encounter him that redefines our definitions of such polar opposites, as well as our assumptions about their interrelation. The assurance also serves as an impetus to explore further what it means for Presbyterians to affirm that Jesus Christ is Lord of the Church. Christ the Donor endows the church and expects that we beneficiaries will follow his intent.

Line 7 begins the second sentence: "It [the Church] belongs to Christ alone." We may sometimes ask, "What does it mean for Presbyterians to follow Christ, to be a disciple, to confess Christ as Lord?" Our *Book of Order* provides responses using general terms, because deciding how *I* will follow Christ, what gifts I have to offer, what I will in fact do, is at the core of personal transformation. The general terms are in effect invitations for each of us to reflect on how we will go about using the gifts we have received.

"Alone" is a key adverb as a preface to the list. The activities identified remind us that in all church life we are beneficiaries of grace, stewards given opportunity for awhile to demonstrate that we are willing stewards, seeking to be faithful. This adverb sets a distinctive tone, later expressed as an implication of God's sovereignty: "the recognition of the human tendency to idolatry and tyranny" (G-2.0500a(4)). Such an expression may sound to some restrictive or cynical. Only when the reference is to Christ alone does it becomes a guide to living responsibly and carefully.

The four infinitives in lines 8–11 outline activities that belong uniquely to Christ as Christ is Head of his body. The first imperative is "to rule." Looking to Scripture, there are three passages that provide background for our understanding, all of which are Jesus' teachings for his disciples during a dispute about primacy. The positive teaching is, "Whoever wishes to be great among you must be your servant" (Matt. 20:26b; cf. Mark 10:43; Luke 22:26). The warning Jesus announces just prior to the foregoing is, "You know that the rulers of the Gentiles lord it over them, and their great ones are tyrants over them. It will not be so among you." The affirmation "Jesus is Lord" carries with it the implication that Jesus reveals how he is Lord, which was a major theme of Jesus' ministry and likely had something to do with why he was crucified.

That Jesus' teaching is to be taken seriously is further emphasized in the following paragraph from the Second Helvetic Confession:

THE POWER OF MINISTERS OF THE CHURCH. Now, therefore, it is fitting that we also say something about the power and duty of the ministers of the Church. Concerning this power some have argued industriously, and to it have subjected everything on earth, even the greatest things, and they have done so contrary to the commandment of the Lord who has prohibited dominion for his disciples and has highly commended humility (Luke 22:24 ff.; Matt. 18:3f.; 20:25ff.). (C-5.157)

The recent discussion of what it means for Presbyterians to say that "Jesus is Lord" has become increasingly shrill, with an increasing tendency not to listen to one another, as well as a stiffening of positions as the wording presented by various protagonists gets increasingly rigid. One wonders how some can allege that the Presbyterian Church (U.S.A.) has departed from its commitment to such a central affirmation of faith when one reflects on how the *Book of Order* begins, especially in this second paragraph. That we see around us evidences of action which call into question whether we are aware of what we are claiming when we make the statement can never be denied, even in our confessions. Still, that paragraph from the mid-sixteenth-century Second Helvetic Confession claimed by us as one of our confessions reassures us even as it challenges how we relate to one another.

Another way of expressing Christ as Lord of the church comes to us from the Westminster Confession:

The purest churches under heaven are subject both to mixture and error: and some have so degenerated as to become apparently no churches of Christ. Nevertheless, there shall be always a Church on earth, to worship God according to his will. (C-6.144)

Jesus as Lord will accomplish his purpose, even when disciples do less than their best in their attempt to follow the Savior. Jesus rules the church, from its beginning to the end of Creation. And the Lord of the church will not let it die, appearances to the contrary notwithstanding. As we sing in Handel's *Messiah*, "And He shall reign forever and ever" (Rev. 11:15).

The second infinitive (line 9) is "to teach." Jesus of Nazareth is frequently considered by many who are not Christians to be the greatest teacher, or at least one of the greatest teachers, in world history. Some have found it easier to call Jesus "Teacher" than to call Jesus "Lord." Virtually every page in the Gospels regarding Jesus' life offers an instance of Jesus' teaching ministry. His early followers called themselves disciples as evidence that they respected Jesus' authority as a teacher. Two Gospels report that when Jesus taught in the synagogue in Capernaum, the reaction of those who heard him was astonishment, since he exuded a unique authority unlike that of anyone they had ever heard previously.[10] This line witnesses to Jesus' authority for our time as well as for that earlier era.

We sometimes wonder what it was that so impressed Jesus' hearers. Such a question is easy to ask, yet impossible to answer outside the circle of faith. Some would suggest that it was the content of Jesus' teaching. Others would offer that it was how he taught. A third possibility is that Jesus' presentation was uniquely transparent to God's truth so that God's Spirit assisted the blending of the content and the method. We are faced with an apparent dilemma, one that we might debate extensively.

With these possible understandings of line 9, we might consider a blending of elements evident in how Scripture describes Jesus as teacher. The content is faithful to the Jesus we know through Scripture. At its best, teaching that consists of parables, where the hearer is challenged to decide about the issues raised, is uniquely consistent with Jesus' style. When a church recognizes that Jesus continues to be the Teacher in this sense, members become disciples, learners, students, discovering at Jesus' feet the way God means for us to live, a way of fellowship and joy.

Line 10 directs us to Jesus as the one who calls. Jesus' authority is distinctive in Jesus' appeal, a way of approaching people where they are offered an opportunity to follow Jesus. This approach is not that of the salesperson seeking to close a deal, but of one who offers an inviting challenge. As the parables stimulate a response in those who hear, based on their own decision, so the call of Jesus Christ across the centuries continues to stimulate seekers to decide on their own who is seeking their obedience.

We Presbyterians struggle with our identification with the doctrine of predestination. How can anyone believe that God chooses those who will be faithful before the world comes into being? It seems ridiculous. We know better, or at least we think we do. There are numerous ways of dealing with this conflict. We Presbyterians must have something wrong.

What may be wrong is that we make this an either/or distinction: either we choose or God chooses. It is not that simple. We choose which church to attend, how we will live out our faith, what we will do as a consequence of these choices. But there is a dimension of our life we do not choose, such as our parents, our nationality, our time. What if matters of faith, how we come to hear about and respond to the gospel of Christ, is more dependent on this latter dimension than we imagine? Then predestination has a different cast.

Such a doctrine also asks us to consider how we understand God, and specifically God's way of dealing with humankind. The God whom Jesus called "Father" because of God's love, is the God who cares for all creation, even that segment which does not return the care. While we affirm that God is all-powerful, we also understand that God's power is always exercised in love, with care for the integrity of those who choose.

The fourth infinitive (line 11) introduces the culmination of G-1.0100b, the object for which the gifts outlined are to be used. Lines 11–14 summarize Christ's purpose for endowing the church. The church is now presented as the instrument God in Christ uses to accomplish God's work in Creation. "Thy kingdom come on earth as it is in heaven" is the warrant as well as the direction for the remaining development of this paragraph. We have here a benchmark for evaluating faithful ministry.

In 2002, Presbyterians restored some traditional language describing the role of the pastor. One of the more troublesome phrases for many was "servants of Christ and stewards of the mysteries of God," from 1 Corinthians 4:1. In the Second Helvetic Confession of 1561, Heinrich Bullinger suggests that the Greek word υπηρετας, "servants," provides a metaphor for how ministers relate to Jesus. He finds in the Greek term for servants another meaning: "rowers." He likens ministers to those who row shells, where they face the back of the shell, taking their directions from the coxswain who alone is facing forward, giving directions to the rowers, in order to make maximum speed and stay on course (C-5.155). What is surprising to me is that such a simple, apt, yet powerful metaphor for ministry is so seldom noticed or discussed in literature about ministry. Bullinger lived long before the song "Turn Your Eyes upon Jesus," but he understood that the admonition was singularly appropriate for ministers, indeed for all the faithful.

The other Greek term, οικονομους, "stewards," reminds us of the theme of this section, the endowed church. The *Book of Order* may be understood as an accountability structure. There are assigned responsibilities for persons and groups. Much of our life together is spent struggling with what those structures are and how they should or should not be applied in specific situations. Some of the animus toward the *Book of Order* may be rooted in just this discomfort with structured accountability. However, ordered life together requires broad agreements, especially when there are large numbers of people involved.

We Presbyterians understand this structure to be penultimate, not the final determiner of destiny. We are all stewards of God's gifts, God's mysteries, accountable, answerable to God finally for how we have conducted our stewardship. The popular notion of judgment on the basis of which sins one has committed, remembering sins of omission as well as sins of commission, disturbs most of us. Even such a sobering prospect, however, is less troubling than the prospect of answering about one's stewardship of God's gifts. I find this latter aspect much more daunting and dreadful—which suggests why such an accounting is seldom mentioned. Yet this is for many where God's grace is most deeply appreciated, where grace becomes the engine of mission.

The English theologian H. H. Farmer suggested that a key aspect of Christian faith could be summed up in a well-known phrase, "grace through personality." Farmer's phrase catches a major theme of Scripture, that God has always chosen people to deliver God's message to those around them. Beginning with Noah, God has chosen men and women to tell those around them of God's intentions. Those chosen have consistently found the responsibility challenging, if not at times almost absurd. The dialogue between God and Moses in Exodus 3 and 4 demonstrates this in a classic sense. Writing from a Jewish perspective, Everett Fox sums up the scene in this way:

> The entire scene is the model for the "call" of the biblical prophet, with its emphasis on God's speaking to the fledgling prophet amid a vision and a motif of refusal: of the call scenes in the Bible, this is the longest and most memorable in its starkness. A man is called by God to return to society and serve as God's spokesperson—despite any opposition he may encounter and

despite his personal shortcomings. Moshe's [Moses'] reluctance, indeed his almost obsessive need to turn down the commission, is as much indicative of the general nature of prophecy . . . as it is of Moshe's own personality.[11]

Fox notes that Moses refuses God's commission five times, and each time God counters the refusal with assurance that Moses will not be left alone without God's help.[12]

It was well into the twentieth century before Protestant churches realized that gender was not a bar to ordained service. We now realize that Scripture offers numerous instances when women provided significant witness to God's power and direction. From Moses' sister Miriam through Esther and Ruth to the Marys of the New Testament, and on to Eunice and Lois, there are numerous evidences in Scripture that God chooses whom God will as messengers. Each of us has received God's grace through women and men in myriad ways. Farmer was correct in his simple expression of how God works through the uniqueness of human beings. And of course we cannot forget that Jesus Christ is preeminent as God's witness. Lines 11–13 might well be understood as restating the priesthood of all believers.

Line 14 recapitulates the purpose of the church's endowment. Now the intent is stated in theological, rather than ecclesiological, language. The focus is the kingdom of God, God's reign over all creation. This is about as close as most Presbyterians get to the doctrine of last things. But here it is, pointing to, establishing, and extending the reign of God.[13]

We live in a time of fascination with God's coming kingdom from many perspectives. Ecologists warn of global warming. Americans have learned that *jihad* is sometimes understood as a warrant for bringing in God's reign through violence. Books portraying how the world will end become bestsellers. The theological term for the violent ending of the world, "apocalypse," has been used for a hit movie, but many people have no awareness that it is a Greek word used in the Bible.

This line in the *Book of Order* points back to the Lord of the kingdom, Jesus Christ. An anchor of an alternative to apocalypse is found in the first three petitions of the Lord's Prayer and their modifier. The well-known petitions are: "*Hallowed* be your name. Your kingdom *come*. Your will *be done*" (emphasis added). The emphasized words are the verbs in the three petitions, strong action words. The subjects of these verbs are your *name*, your *kingdom*, your *will*. All this is familiar.

What is less understood is how all three petitions are modified by the phrase "on earth as it is in heaven." The model is not something humans develop, but how God has already established God's rule. Jesus' parables about God's kingdom demonstrate that the way disciples go about their role in establishing and extending that kingdom is through quiet, yet consistent faithfulness.

What is surprising about the final lines of this paragraph is that the focus is not on the Presbyterian Church (U.S.A.), but on God's kingdom. The endowment is not a denominational strategy, but an understanding that our task is contributing to the establishment and extension of God's rule on earth for all humankind. The endowment is not for us Presbyterians, but for all God's children of every time and place.

Finding Christ

The section ends by pointing beyond Presbyterian structures and processes. However well we comply with our polity, there is always that superior vision, when God will fulfill God's purpose for all creation. We properly serve in our order to the extent that we convey the gospel of Jesus Christ about God's liberating and empowering love. The question is how we get from this endowment to the church in which we live.

Notes

1. For a careful discussion of how to deal with this situation, see James Hudnut-Beumler, "Creating a Commonwealth: The History, Theology, and Ethics of Church Endowments." This address to the National Association of Endowed Presbyterian Churches (October 18, 1996) is available at www.peernetwork.org.

2. Ibid., p. 7.

3. Ibid., p. 9.

4. See *Book of Confessions* 5.124: "But because God from the beginning would have men [*sic*] to be saved, and to come to the knowledge of the truth, it is altogether necessary that there always should have been, and should be now, and to the end of the world, a Church." See also 6.140, as well as 3.18.

5. Mark Kraai, "Spoiled Manna," *New Brunswick Theological Seminary Alumniae Alert*, January 2002.

6. W. F. Albright and C. S. Mann, *Matthew*, vol. 26 of *The Anchor Bible* (Garden City, NY: Doubleday & Co., 1981), p. 74. Their discussion of the petition refers to Ex. 16:22ff.

7. *Book of Common Worship—Daily Prayer* (Louisville, Ky.: Westminster/John Knox Press, 1993), p. 245. Other Scripture allusions are to Phil. 2:10 and Rev. 19:9.

8. Emphasis added. Other instances are *Book of Confessions* 3.18; 4.026, .030; 5.114; 6.006; 7.239.

9. Gerhard Friedrich, ed., *Theological Dictionary of the New Testament*, vol. 4 (Grand Rapids: Wm. B. Eerdmans Publishing Co., 1967), p. 65. Strathmann argues persuasively that this word in Scripture always has a sacrificial sense, notably in the temptation narratives in Matthew 4:10 and Luke 4:8.

10. Mark 1:22 and Luke 4:32. Luke suggests that this authority was emerging when Jesus as a twelve-year-old amazes teachers in the Jerusalem Temple (2:46).

11. Everett Fox, *The Five Books of Moses* (New York: Schocken Books, 1983). From notes on Exodus 3:1–4:17, p. 268. Fox's remark about call scenes in the Hebrew Bible is equally true of instances of "call" in the New Testament.

12. Ibid.

13. See chapter 4, where G-1.0300d offers an eschatological view.

1. *Christ gives to his Church*
2. *its faith and life,*
3. *its unity and mission,*
4. *its officers and ordinances.*
5. *Insofar as Christ's will for the Church*
6. *is set forth in Scripture,*
7. *it is to be obeyed.*
8. *In the worship and service of God*
9. *and the government of the church,*
10. *matters are to be ordered*
11. *according to the Word*
12. *by reason and sound judgment,*
13. *under the guidance of the Holy Spirit.*

(G-1.0100c)

3

Two Formulas and the Prime Directive

The first chapter of the *Book of Order* begins with Creation, then with a succinct yet powerful commentary on the Christ hymn of Philippians 2:5–11, establishing a Christological basis for what is to follow. The second paragraph discusses Christ's continuing relationship with the church, presented in terms of his continuing action as well as his authority for those in the church. This discussion sets forth a general, abstract, yet pertinent outline for church life.

With G-1.0100c, the third paragraph, we turn to church life in the present. On the foundation set forth, derived from Scripture, what sort of guidance is there for Presbyterians seeking to be faithful? How do we go about our ministry, our service, our discipleship? How can we find our way amid the complexities of modern life, as well as the diversity of perspectives that emerge in our life together? Are there any core values for Presbyterians? If so, what are they? These urgent questions require response.

We find two formulas in these thirteen lines, bracketing an assertion meant to be definitive guidance for those seeking direction. *Formula* is a word we usually associate with mathematics, the science whose letters and special signs either excite or intimidate us. The word is also used in a more general sense, indicating some degree of complex relationships among various concepts. It in this latter sense that *formula* appears in the title for this section.

Living in a complex world, we experience a general uneasiness with complex printed material. The pace of life invites us always to speed up, to get things done, to meet the schedule. The gift of a formula is a way to keep our path defined and relatively clear, determining our priorities. We begin to learn that while the pace of life entices, its allure is a challenge regarding who or what we allow to be in charge of our lives. Formulas enable us to reorder our lives.

Formula 1

G-1.0100c begins with Christ as the subject of the sentence, as does the previous paragraph. Christ is the subject of the faith of the church. The verb is surprising: "Christ gives." The verb is present tense, because the sentence is about an ongoing, present reality. Christ in the present actively continues as head of the church. Christ, the One who has given us so much through his life, death, and resurrection, continues to give today, for Christ is the same yesterday, today, and forever.

This first formula lists six gifts Christ gives to the church. These gifts are conjoined, rather than merely listed. The list is presented in a way that suggests a dynamic between the terms in each pair. The simple word *and* repeated in each pair adds support for reflection on how each pair is developed.

This pairing brings to mind a time when my dad brought me two magnets. I was fascinated by their action. Held one way, they attracted each other and I could feel it as they snapped together. Reversing one of them meant that they could not get together. This new situation gave me a different feeling, the reverse effect of magnetism. Unless the two magnets were put together just so, the result was repelling rather than attracting. The gifts paired here belong together, but need to be brought together.

The first pair appears in line 2: "its [the Church's] faith and life." Some Presbyterians recall how the first series of major new church school curriculum materials was called *Christian Faith and Life*. Designed while the Second World War was winding down, it was initially considered an outrageous and extravagant enterprise.[1] Those materials were the fresh start for which Presbyterians were waiting. Their integrity and challenge were eventually copied by other denominations, thus proving their vigor.

Conjoining *faith* and *life* as a pair of gifts that Christ gives the church suggests that these two belong together. Both the faith of the church and the life of the church come from Christ, together with major challenges. We are so eager to claim the faith for ourselves, convinced that our view is correct, that others seem sometimes less devoted or less perceptive than we are. Such conclusions indicate that we have forgotten that the faith we profess is a gift from our Lord and Savior. No matter how careful we are, the faith we profess can never be the same as the faith once delivered to the church and continually revivified by God's gracious spirit. Each of us receives the gift of faith as we are, the product of our biological, historical, social, and intellectual heritage. Each of us hears the Word differently to one degree or another. The miracle is that the gift of faith comes and binds us to others into a community that seeks to be faithful to the Giver of faith.

As Christ gives the church its faith, so also Christ gives life to the church. Pairing faith and life reminds us that as faith takes root and grows within us, it is continually interacting with how we live, how we perceive our surroundings, how we respond to the opportunities and challenges that come to us. The challenge is to maintain an awareness that both faith and life are gifts from Christ.

Living with that awareness is like holding the magnets; sometimes they pull together, sometimes they seem to be flying apart, each wanting to go its own way. The latter is by far the most distressing and painful. Yet such times often become, in retrospect, periods when our faith and understanding have grown beyond what we could have imagined. Such is the life of the believer.

Such is the life and faith of the church, and especially within a particular church or presbytery or denomination. Open any chapter in the history of the Presbyterian Church and the pains are evident. The elder who characterized the *Book of Order* as having "blood on every page" appreciated what he found because of the difficult situation in which his church currently found itself.[2] All of us carry within us a hope that the church will be in fact "the provisional demonstration of what God intends for all humanity" (G-3.0200). Yet, with the medieval monk, we learn that a too-apt metaphor is Noah's ark, where we couldn't stand the mess on the inside were it not for the chaos on the outside.[3] While there is always a deep sense that "it shouldn't be this way," there are times and seasons when it is. We know from the psalms of lament that such awareness can be excruciatingly painful. We eventually understand that nostalgia for "the way we wish things to be" takes energy away from being about God's work in the real world.

The challenge is to accept that faith and life are both gifts from Christ to us, for our proper stewardship of thanksgiving. As we accept this affirmation about our own lives we begin to affirm that the life of the church is similarly a gift, that Christ is providing for faith and life even amid whatever dark clouds appear at the moment to darken such a view.

Confessing with the Gospel of John that "the Word became flesh and lived among us" (John 1:14) implies that we who follow the One who was the Word will always live lives of paradox, at least as long as we belong to the Church Militant.[4] The *Book of Order* may be seen as reminding the church of the dilemmas that confront the faithful through the ages. These recurring dilemmas need to be reconsidered periodically in the light of the church's experience, and resolved again somewhat differently than the previous time. This is our heritage from the Reformation.[5]

The pairing of faith and life suggests that these two must be kept together in the church one way or another. Certain ways of focusing on faith as doctrine risk removing from consideration the balancing, and at times opposing, awareness of the liveliness of the fellowship. The decision in 1967 to expand our *Book of Confessions* beyond the documents from Westminster is one instance where our church sought to recognize and act in response to the challenge of the church's historicity.[6] The church's faith and life are both gifts being given the church.

Line 3 designates another pair of gifts, "unity and mission." One of the major ironies of American Presbyterian history is that these two concerns have been at the heart of much dissension in the Presbyterian family. Often it has been the gift of mission that has triggered disagreement, as well as actual division. Nor is this a recent phenomenon.

A division between the Old Side and the New Side of the Presbyterian Church occurred in 1741. The church had come into being in 1706 with the forming of the first presbytery, which then became a synod in 1729. While as usual there were various areas of disagreement, a major issue had to do with how pastors fulfilled their preaching responsibility. To read the minutes of both the Synod of Philadelphia and the Synod of New York in 1744 after they had divided is to encounter the pain as well as the fervent conviction of both sides that their choice in dividing the Presbyterian Church had been necessary.[7]

Another major issue involved itinerant preachers. The view of the Synod of Philadelphia on the practice of itinerant preachers is clear from a portion of their first minutes:

> We think that to give any minister a right to preach in any brother's pulpit contrary to his inclination, without presbyterial order for that purpose, is the direct way to breed and foment divisions and quench brotherly love among ministers. . . . Besides we think that itinerant preaching properly so called (i.e., when preaching is the principal [reason] for travel) except by express order of the presbytery, hath no foundation in the word of God. Even Paul and Barnabas had a particular order for their traveling among the Gentiles.[8]

This division lasted until reunion in 1758, when the two synods united as the Synod of New York and Philadelphia. An indication that the issue of itinerant preaching continued to be a bone of contention is shown in part by the fifth heading in the Plan for Reunion:

> And it shall be considered in the same view [a censurable evil] if any presbytery appoint supplies in the bounds of another presbytery, without their concurrence; or if any member officiate in another's congregation, without asking and obtaining his consent; or the session's, in case the minister be absent: yet it shall be esteemed unbrotherly for any one, in ordinary circumstances, to refuse his consent to a regular member, when it is requested.[9]

This compromise by the two synods continues to affect our life together as Presbyterians. For instance, G-14.0606 regarding former staff officiating at services in a church is to be "only upon invitation from the moderator of the session or, in case of the inability to contact the moderator, from the clerk of session." Authorization for service to a particular church has similar limitations (G-14.0307).[10]

The major disruption of Presbyterian life in the nineteenth century was the Old School–New School controversy, which began in 1837 and continued to 1870. It has been said that the root of this division was the compromise of 1758, that the tension between unity and mission had only been temporarily settled. The earlier problems were complicated by the explosion of immigration into the "West," which meant Ohio and Kentucky.

Missionary societies began to be formed by many denominations, including the Presbyterians in 1789, when the first General Assembly requested that each synod recommend to the next meeting "two members well qualified to be employed in missions on our frontier."[11] Twenty-one years later the General Assembly identified four priorities for mission: "gospelizing the Indians; instructing the negroes [*sic*]; distributing Bibles, books, and tracts; educating young men for the ministry."[12] The "invention" of mission societies as a response to immigration was not limited to Presbyterians or to denominational structures.

Presbyterians agreed in 1801 to a Plan of Union with Congregationalists. *Union* did not mean then what it has come to mean today. It was a comity agreement, that in the new areas whichever church was organized first would be accepted as valid. The other body would not form a competing congregation until the community had grown to a certain size. This strategy combining unity and mission seemed effective for a while, and then problems arose. People from churches organized under the Plan of Union were called Presbygationalists, not a complimentary term.[13]

Regarding the schism of 1837–38, J. A. Hodge wrote in 1907, "The origin of the trouble dated as far back as the Plan of Union formed with the General Association of Connecticut."[14] He identified eight "chief causes" of separation:

1. Diversities of doctrinal beliefs.
2. Practical modifications of the "Form of Government."
3. The dissolution of "elective affinity"[15] courts.
4. Application and methods of discipline.
5. Changes in forms of worship.
6. The abrogation of the Plan of Union and the disowning of the Synods and Presbyteries formed under it.
7. The influence exerted over our missionaries and our church courts by organizations for church work independent of all ecclesiastical jurisdiction, even of the General Assembly.
8. Manner of educating Candidates [*sic*].[16]

Notice that abolition of slavery does not appear in this list. Others have proposed other reasons for the schism, to the extent that no single or main cause can be identified.[17]

Item 3 in Hodge's list, "The dissolution of 'elective affinity' courts" was the action taken by the General Assembly in 1837. After two attempts at reconciliation failed, the General Assembly voted 132–105 to cut off or excind the four synods of Western Reserve, Utica, Geneva, and Genesee from the General Assembly. All four were the "elective affinity" synods. "Five other synods—New Jersey, Albany, Cincinnati, Illinois, and Michigan—were admonished to take order on the doctrinal errors within their bounds, and report in writing to the next assembly."[18]

Patton reports that the pastor of Brick Presbyterian Church in New York City, Dr. Gardiner Spring, among many others, lamented the way in which the excision took place.[19] It is a sad irony that this same pastor in May 1861 authored a resolution restricting membership in the Old School General Assembly that year to those who would "acknowledge and declare their obligation . . . to preserve our beloved Union unimpaired."[20] Thus, there came about another division of Presbyterians, one that lasted until 1983.

The division that took place in the twentieth century was yet again an instance where unity was fractured over mission concerns, as indicated in a recent article titled

"The Crisis of Foreign Missions."[21] This crisis came to a head when the book by William Ernest Hocking and others, *Re-Thinking Missions: A Laymen's Inquiry After One Hundred Years,* appeared in 1932,[22] challenging many of the cherished understandings of mission that had stood for decades. A vigorous reaction to this volume was written by J. Gresham Machen, who had left his position as assistant professor of New Testament at Princeton Theological Seminary in 1929 for the newly formed Westminster Seminary in Philadelphia. In a memorandum in January 1933, Machen wrote his view that *Re-Thinking Missions*

> constitutes from beginning to end an attack upon the historic Christian faith. It presents as the aim of missions that of *seeking* truth together with adherents of other religions rather than that of *presenting* the truth which God has supernaturally recorded in the Bible.[23]

When such concerns failed to convince the 1933 General Assembly, Machen and H. McAllister Griffiths announced a committee of twenty-five to form what became the Independent Board of Foreign Missions, headquartered on the outskirts of Philadelphia.[24]

The 1934 General Assembly directed

> that all ministers and laymen affiliated with the Presbyterian Church U. S. A. who are officers, trustees, or members of the "Independent Board of Presbyterian Foreign Missions" sever their connection with the Board.[25]

Further, the General Assembly directed that presbyteries should institute disciplinary proceedings against those who refused to obey the decision regarding this new entity. Machen, who was found guilty of six charges and suspended from office "until such time as he shall give satisfactory evidence of repentance,"[26] appealed to synod, then to the General Assembly. In not sustaining any of the twelve specifications of error in the Machen case, the Permanent Judicial Commission went on to summarize the essential question to be this:

> If a minister or member of the Church is dissatisfied with an authorized agency of the Church, has he a right to organize an agency according to his own views, in competition with the Church's agency, and meanwhile to claim his rights under the Church's Constitution?

The answer was no, and especially when "his denunciations of fellow ministers and of members of the church to which he belonged, amounting to defamation of character, which are found in the record, seriously aggravated his other offenses."[27] Subsequently, Machen and others formed another denomination, to be called the Orthodox Presbyterian Church.[28]

This review of our history demonstrates the ongoing tension between mission and unity within our denomination. The threat of schism is seldom far from

Presbyterian awareness. Small wonder that often the months leading up to General Assembly are filled with speculation about whether this is the year we will split.

Such a sad history suggests that we have historically understood unity and mission to be things we control, rather than qualities given to us by Christ the Lord. We tend to forget that these two apparently competing realities of church life are, according to our *Book of Order*, gifts from the Lord of the church, not programs of a local Presbyterian church, or a presbytery, or a synod, or even of a unit of the General Assembly Council. The reality of the mission Jesus Christ gives to the church is far more complex and complicated, even diverse, than we are willing to admit. How can we affirm the diversity of gifts about which Paul writes and at the same time insist that "my" view of mission, even when I have lots of others who agree with me, is "the" mission to which everyone should be committed?

Can "our" mission be a celebration of the gifts of the many serving the Savior as they are called and gifted? Can we find a measure of unity that energizes us to fuller obedience to the Lord of the church than to the party spirit which argues that "our" view is the only view which is faithful to Jesus? Can we find a way to work together for the sake of Christ's kingdom, rather than merely to demonstrate that separately we are at least true to our perception of what Christ intends?

The third pair of gifts, found in line 4, also startles us, this time because they are unexpected gifts. The gifts are "officers" and "ordinances." These are simple nouns, but they carry with them various understandings.

It is surprising that the collective noun given in the *Book of Order* for officers is so seldom used today. That noun is *presbyters*, coming from the Greek word for elder (G-6.0103). This term enters the biblical record in Exodus 3:18; hence it is a term with a rich history for the people of the Bible. How odd that we use "Presbyterian" to name ourselves, yet find it difficult to say the word by which we are known. We Presbyterians assert that both ministers and elders are presbyters and both are called to ministry (G-6.0105), and that a balance of ministers and elders is required in governing bodies above the session. When we adopt the "lay and clergy" distinction, we undercut the assertion about presbyters. Some might conclude that "fitting in" with the language of those around us has replaced honoring heritage.

Some groups of Christians would find the assertion that officers are a gift of Christ to the church an erroneous one, and beyond understanding. Since the Reformation of the sixteenth century, some groups have come together as a conventicle without leaders, practicing pure democracy. Martin Luther's understanding of the "priesthood of all believers" became the stimulus for these groups to adopt a radical understanding of that principle.

Sociologists of religion call such groups *acephalous*, having no head. Yet some of their studies show that patterns of leadership quickly emerge behind the scenes when someone begins to organize details of such a community's life. It appears that people need leaders when they gather to execute any purpose, a reality that Calvin noted.[29]

The *Book of Order* chapter on "The Church and Its Officers" echoes line 4 with its introduction: "All ministry in the Church is a gift from Jesus Christ" (G-6.0101).

The scriptural pattern for Presbyterian ministry also comes with the gift: "not to be served but to serve."[30]

In 1811 Samuel Miller preached a sermon titled "The Divine Appointment, the Duties, and the Qualifications of Elders."[31] After commenting that some regard elders as the result only of "human prudence alone," which he terms an "erroneous view," Miller comments:

> We are by no means, then, to consider ruling elders as a mere ecclesiastical convenience, or as a set of counsellors whom the wisdom of [hu]man[s] alone has chosen, and who may, therefore, be reverenced and obeyed as little or as much as human caprice may think proper; but as bearing an office of divine appointment—as the "ministers of God for good" to his church—and whose lawful and regular acts ought to command our conscientious obedience.[32]

Fewer elders than ministers of the Word and Sacrament consider themselves "Christ's gift to the Church." Such a self-understanding is both daunting and dangerous. It is daunting when officers realize that their task is "to seek together to find and represent the will of Christ" (G-4.0301d). Miller's understanding gives pause to every elder who considers the meaning of being an elder. To be an officer once was called an awesome responsibility. It is still daunting when we consider the role of those ordained to office in the Presbyterian Church.

It is also a dangerous consideration, if becoming an officer is not deeply appreciated. G-4.0301d includes the important word "together." The servant role reminds officers that they are called to work as a team, to be concerned that all work to serve the Lord they confess, who has called them to this responsibility. Each one comes bringing the gifts and abilities given to him or her by God, for building up the body of Christ.

The discussion of offices in the sixth chapter of the *Book of Order* explains how the variety of skills and training are intended to work together. Serving the Lord of the church enables the various people with their diverse talents and perspectives to build up the church. This sense of cooperation is emphasized repeatedly in the *Book of Order*, especially in the discussion of how the three types of officers are meant to work together. A key word in this discussion is "with," emphasizing the cooperative spirit essential for fulfilling the responsibilities of office. The line we consider does use the plural form, "officers."

Mutuality is expressed even in details. When an elder or deacon wishes to resign from active service, it requires "the session's consent" (G-14.0210). Similarly, when a minister wishes to dissolve a pastoral relationship with a particular church, the relationship "may be dissolved only by presbytery" (G-14.0601).[33] Such complexity runs counter to the way most other organizations conduct their affairs.

This requisite and detailed mutuality protects us from the dangers of those serving the church. Our brothers and sisters work with us, reminding us of our commitments and our calling. I have concluded that one bumper sticker–type comment for being Presbyterian is, "We get by with a lot of help from our friends."

The Presbyterian corollary to our central affirmation of God's sovereignty is a "recognition of the human tendency to . . . tyranny" (G-2.0500a(4)). We work together both to provide mutual support in our wrestling with how to be faithful witnesses to God's power in Jesus Christ, and to alert one another to tendencies toward "thinking of ourselves more highly than we ought to think."

It is crucial to keep this understanding of covenant mutuality alive during times of controversy. Presbyterians have been prone to escalate rhetoric amid stressful situations, which has occasionally led to separation, as noted earlier. Is this perhaps due to our tendency to value our individual identity more than our being baptized into a covenant fellowship?

One Presbyterian value has been our commitment to education, an emphasis rooted in Calvin's Geneva, where he organized a school so that everyone would be able to read broadly. The longest chapter in the *Book of Order* is *G-14.0000*, where we find the process by which church members become officers. Elders are supposed to be prepared for service through study, followed by examination by the session before their ordination and installation (G-14.0205). Compliance with this provision varies widely, from rigorous to nonexistent.

The allegation that elder commissioners to governing bodies are manipulated in their voting by minister commissioners and staff reflects a distressing diminution of the role of elders. Samuel Miller wrote,

> In the church session, . . . every member has an equal voice. The vote of the most humble and retiring ruling elder is of the same avail as that of his minister, so that no pastor can carry any measure unless he can obtain the concurrence of a majority of the eldership.[34]

The insistence on equality of elders and ministers in governing bodies above the session extends this high regard for the elder, who must be persuaded that a proposal merits approval.[35]

Officers, especially elders, are Christ's gifts to the church. They are much more than warm bodies to fill slots on a board, names on a list. Accepting ordination is a serious step, too seldom emphasized. It is committing one's talents and abilities to the service of Christ in a specific place, being willing to labor with one's colleagues in ministry to God's greater glory in Jesus Christ, using those gifts God has given to each for the good of all.

The other term in line 4, "ordinances," is not a word associated with church. Most of us are more accustomed to understanding ordinances to be what city councils pass. We see the word on signs telling us what we can't do—unless we are willing to pay a fine for our action. Town governments pass many ordinances about what can and can't be done in their jurisdiction. Approval of the city budget and the resulting tax rate are called ordinances.

What could "ordinances" mean in the Presbyterian *Book of Order?* The Westminster Larger Catechism gives both a definition and a list of ordinances when it considers the duties required in the Second Commandment:

the receiving, observing, and keeping pure and entire, all such religious
worship and ordinances as God hath instituted in his Word; particularly
prayer and thanksgiving in the name of Christ;
the reading, preaching, and hearing of the Word;
the administration and receiving of the sacraments;
church government and discipline;
the ministry and maintenance thereof;
religious fasting;
swearing by the name of God; and vowing unto him. (C-7.218).[36]

A more recent, somewhat expanded list of ordinances appeared in the *Book of
Church Order* of the former Presbyterian Church (U.S.):

prayer;
the singing of psalms and hymns;
reading, expounding, and preaching the Word of God;
administering the Sacraments of Baptism and the Lord's Supper;
fasting and thanksgiving;
catechising;
Christian nurture;
making offerings for the relief of the poor, the extension of the Gospel, and
other Christian causes;
exercising discipline; and,
invoking the blessing of God upon the people.[37]

An alternate way of describing these ten activities is "the means of grace," in the
sense of how God's grace comes to the community of faith. This list summarizes the
contents of the Directory for Worship in our *Book of Order*.

The word *ordinances* derives from the word *order*. Consequently, God's ordinances are those provisions God has made whereby God's grace becomes evident
and lively in the church.[38] Some of the items in this list may strike us as out of place.
Such questioning might broaden our understanding of God's provision for us, appreciating that all these are encompassed in the designation of Christ's gifts to the church.

Fasting is not something usually understood as a means of grace. Giving up
some food for Lent has become a virtual joke for many. Dieting is considered an almost
insurmountable hurdle for those who are burdened with more weight than is healthy.
But when we consider fasting as a means of grace, our understanding of this spiritual
discipline (the contemporary way of speaking of the "means of grace") is transformed.

Another word in the list of "ordinances" that seems totally out of place at first
glance is *discipline*. The Preamble to the Rules of Discipline suggests a transformed
understanding of this troublesome word, both in terms of what it means as well as
what it does not mean:

The power that Jesus Christ has vested in his Church, a power manifested in the exercise of church discipline, is one for building up the body of Christ, not for destroying it, for redeeming, not for punishing. It should be exercised as a dispensation of mercy and not of wrath so that the great ends of the Church may be achieved, that all children of God may be presented faultless in the day of Christ. (D-1.0102)

Many Presbyterians do not know that there are Rules of Discipline. Many of those who are aware of the process do not understand its purpose, especially as defined in this paragraph. The rules themselves underline their significance by requiring that this statement be read at the outset of every trial.[39]

This historic listing of ordinances, or means of grace, has generally been forgotten. The periodic liturgical revivals have reintroduced many of these spiritual disciplines, which are rooted in Scripture. The result has been that these spiritual disciplines are often understood as personal disciplines, done by an individual who accepts responsibility to follow some of these exercises. The Presbyterian tradition has located these in church life as what the community does as a disciplined fellowship. "Ordinances" carries with it the sense that these are community activities, ordered for the health of the church of Jesus Christ.

Pairing "ordinances" with "officers" offers us an intriguing juxtaposition. The connecting of these two gifts reminds Presbyterians of our conviction about ordination to function.[40] Ordinances are the concern and responsibility of officers. Conversely, officers are faithful in their office only to the degree that they are aware of these responsibilities. It should be more widely understood that effective officers are faithful to the degree that their work is pursued as a means of grace for the church. The sad emergence of business techniques as primary criteria for how our life together in the church is conducted has led increasingly for calls to reinstate an understanding that church administration is first of all a divine gift, that an M.B.A. or certification of professional skill in management is an important and helpful, yet secondary, additional skill.

As the discussion of the first formula closes, it is well to recall that the eight gifts of Christ to the church that we have considered are in fact mutually related. A visual representation would be an octagon with a gift at each corner, joined to all the others in a dynamic, interacting system. That is a different way of describing how our life together as Presbyterian Christians is meant to function. Such complexity introduced at the outset of the *Book of Order* prepares us for the complexity that follows. It also alerts us to the challenge of being faithful as disciples of the One who provides such bounty for us.

This leads us to ask, "What then are we to do?"

The Prime Directive

The television series *Star Trek* contributed the phrase "prime directive" to our language. The Federation required commitment of all its starships that when they "made contact with a developing society, they [would] do nothing to interfere with the natural progress of that culture."[41] Such a directive became a major plot device in the series, with the crew of the *Enterprise* continually wrestling with the dilemmas resulting from this principle of space exploration.

What prime directive has the Lord of the church given us? This is a continuing question for all Christians. Presbyterians in the United States since 1727 have used the phrase "essential tenets" to express the core of our faith. This phrase appears in the questions asked when elders and ministers are ordained: "Do you sincerely receive and adopt the essential tenets of the Reformed faith as expressed in the confessions of our church as authentic expressions of what Scripture leads us to believe and do?" (G-14.0207c; G-14.0405b(3)). Ordaining bodies examine on this basis, and each one determines what the phrase means.

In 1920 the General Assembly attempted to provide a definitive understanding of the phrase by accepting the so-called "five fundamentals" as required for ordination. A Special Commission, called the Swearingen Commission after its chairman, was appointed in 1925 to consider whether the 1910 action was correct. In its lengthy report in 1927, it reported regarding the 1910 action:

> It was clearly the intention that this decision as to essential and necessary articles was to be made after the candidate had been presented and had declared his beliefs and stated his motives personally, and after the examining body, whether Presbytery or (General) Synod, had had full opportunity to judge the man himself, as well as abstract questions of doctrine.[42]

"Essential tenets" continues to generate debate and controversy among Presbyterians for whom ambiguity is considered foreign to our fellowship.

"Prime directive" offers an alternative, focusing more on what it is we are about, rather than what we must believe to be appropriately Presbyterian. It poses the challenge to consider what is at the heart of being Presbyterian.

This introduction suggests how important lines 5–7 are. I submit that the Presbyterian prime directive is located in the middle sentence of G-1.0100c, lines 5–7, as set out at the beginning of this chapter. The first two words of this prime directive are "insofar as," an adverbial phrase suggesting both a basic understanding, and a limit beyond which further direction is necessary. "Insofar as" is like a blinking yellow light at an intersection, noting that caution is strongly advisable even when proceeding. We are alerted and made aware of decisions to be made, a challenge with which to wrestle.

This adverbial phrase identifies "Christ's will for the Church" as the topic under discussion, hence the designation "prime directive," which helps us understand what this sentence is about. Note that it is about "Christ's will," what Christ wants the church to be and do. This is at the heart of why we have a *Book of Order*.

The prime directive is to obey Christ's will for the Church "as set forth in Scripture." But unfortunately that isn't a simple process: which command of Jesus do we follow? Let us look at the following three possible texts as an experiment:

A. The Great Commandment: Matthew 22:32–40; Mark 12:28–34; Luke 10:25–28. "You shall love the Lord your God with all your heart, and with all your soul, and with all your mind." [And] "You shall love your neighbor as yourself."

B. A New Commandment: John 13:34. "I give you a new commandment, that you love one another . . . as I have loved you."

C. The Great Commission: Matthew 28:19–20. "Go therefore and make disciples of all nations, baptizing them in the name of the Father and of the Son and of the Holy Spirit, and teaching them to obey everything that I have commanded you."

Must we choose one of these? A and B are both about love in a particular sense. Does C imply "love"? If it did, there would be some consistency, and we might have a starting place.

We are commanded to love in both A and B. There is a distinctive word for love in the Greek for which we have no single word in English. It is central in both the A and B passages. John's version (B) is instructive, in that we are to love as God in Christ has loved us. This suggests that we are ordered to combine forgiveness and gratitude, especially toward those who are, according to most standards, unworthy of our attention.[43] This echoes the discussion in chapter 2 about the association of gratitude with the exodus experience as well as the resurrection of Jesus Christ. Jesus Christ as Lord is the norm for life in the church.

How can we be commanded to love, much less to love as Jesus loved us? Nearly two centuries ago Søren Kierkegaard, in a sermon on Matthew 22:39, offered as the "criterion of the Christian love and its characteristic, that it contains the apparent contradiction, *that loving is a duty*."[44] The Danish theologian went on to wonder at the immensity of such a commandment:

> What courage was not needed in order to say for the first time, "Thou shalt love," or rather, what divine authority was not needed in order by this word to reverse the ideas and concepts of natural man [*sic*]! For there at the border line where human language pauses and courage weakens, there the revelation breaks forth with divine primitiveness and proclaims what is not difficult to understand in the sense of requiring depth of understanding or human parallels, but which nevertheless does not originate in any human heart. It is not really difficult to understand when it has been said, and it only wishes to be understood in order to be obeyed.[45]

Kierkegaard finds that the commandment to love is a witness to the authority of Jesus Christ.

A more contemporary German scholar ponders another word that he suggests is the hallmark of the Christian community. Gerhard Lohfink points out that an overlooked word in the New Testament is the reciprocal pronoun "one another," which is found in B.[46] Lohfink identifies this designation as the hallmark of community. He points out that the apostle Paul uses this pronoun forty times in his epistles. He further points out that these are mostly admonitions, exhorting the recipients to treat one another as a community of forgiveness. Some of the examples he cites are:

> outdo one another in showing honor (Rom. 12:10)
> live in harmony with one another (Rom. 12:16)
> admonish one another (Rom. 15:14)
> wait for one another (1 Cor. 11:33)
> bear one another's burdens (Gal. 6:2)
> build one another up (1 Thess. 5:11)
> be at peace with one another (1 Thess. 5:13)[47]

Lohfink suggests that such mutuality should be the hallmark of the church. He cites Galatians 3:28 to remind us how Paul took Jesus' teaching and applied it to the increasing diversity of the early Christian church. Cultural distinctions of nationality, civil distinctions, and gender were transcended with the oneness associated with being "in Christ."

The third form of the Great Commission, identified above as C, is better known than the other two, but has sometimes had an unfortunate effect in the history of our faith. The English translation of the verb "to make disciples" has periodically led some to justify the use of coercive or manipulative strategies. There have been periods where "making disciples" has justified methods that oppose the spirit of loving devotion implicit in A and B forms. Some groups use the verb form "discipling" in an attempt to retain the spirit of willing commitment consistent with the New Testament witness.

We Presbyterians like to say that "Theology matters." Sometimes, however, we think "doctrine" when we say "theology." Our tendency is to focus on a specific doctrine that seems at the time more pertinent than others. How can we escape from this fascination with specific doctrines without sacrificing our reasoned quest for faith?

We seek to be obedient to our Lord whose teachings we revere. Yet we are faced with the challenge of determining what we must do to fulfill our discipleship. What sounds so simple leads us into additional questions. We are faithful seekers, open to direction, as we deal with emerging challenges for which we are unprepared.

As with the starship *Enterprise*, the prime directive articulates a principle, while pressing us into new situations where "new occasions teach new duties."[48]

"Prime directive" is a contemporary way of referring to the Reformation principle of "Scripture alone." The Reformers used this motto as a way of referring to their quest for faithfulness to what Jesus had commanded his disciples during his life with them. Such a focus led them to teach that there were only two sacraments, Baptism and the Lord's Supper. The church previously had held that there were seven.

Many Protestants today think that the phrase made popular by Billy Graham, "The Bible says . . . ," is the sum total of "Scripture alone." All one needs to do is to find a verse of Scripture, and this becomes the basis for action consistent with the faith of the Bible. The prime directive corrects this understanding by expressing that it is the commandments of Jesus Christ that are determinative.

The challenge of re-forming churches raised the question of how disciples were to order their life together. In Acts 6, the need to organize to handle community issues emerges for the early church, and elders are mentioned.[49] But there is also the word for bishop, or overseer.[50] The challenge for the Reformers and for Protestants since their time have been two passages, 1 Timothy 3:2 and Titus 1:5–9. These are significant passages for Presbyterians, since we have taken the Greek word for elder as the way we are known.

Formula 2: The Quadrate Formula

I've chosen the word *quadrate* as a way to emphasize that the next lines of G-1.0100c present four interrelated considerations that need to be carefully understood both individually and together. It is a not a formula in either a mathematical or a scientific sense. The expression presents a complex of four elements, related to each another in such a way that putting them together produces a satisfactory result. This quadrate formula is a corollary of the prime directive, acknowledging that Scripture doesn't provide direct information about how worship should be conducted, or about how churches should organize their affairs. Lines 8–9 demonstrate this acknowledgment by beginning the next sentence with the phrase "in the worship and service of God and the government of the church."

A small but significant shift occurs when we read this phrase: for the first time in the three paragraphs, the word *church* is *not* capitalized. The discussion has moved from considering how our Lord relates to all believers everywhere in all times and places, to a specific community of faith. We move from theological affirmations to the need to derive the details of life in a community from those affirmations and what is involved in particularizing a church community. The Word of God in Scripture needs to become fleshed out with the details of community life.

The significance of this transition often gets lost as Presbyterians talk to one another. There is a tendency for us to think "church" in terms of its transhistorical, transnational, transconfessional sense, when we should be thinking "church" as a particular aspect of the larger whole. When these two understandings are not kept distinct, the tendency is to escalate the rhetoric in our discussions and debates. We require carefully prescribed theological bifocals lest we stumble into disputes made unresolvable by our inability to keep in mind this important distinction.

Such caution introduces us to a formula from the Reformation that is seldom articulated as clearly as it is here in G-1.001c. Professor John Leith, discussing "theology as dialogue" in an epilogue to his book on the Westminster Assembly, writes, "The theological dialogue is simply the attempt to articulate in clear, precise, and coherent terms the meaning and purpose of human existence for those who believe that ultimate Reality has been finally disclosed in Jesus of Nazareth."[51] Leith summarizes his book suggesting that "The Westminster Confession can best be understood as an episode in the continuing dialogue of Christian theology."[52]

The scope of this formula is limited by the introduction in lines 8–9 to three areas of church life. The first two are paired: the worship and service[53] of God. Worship and service are inextricably joined. Such a juxtaposition is found also in G-2.0100b, where the role of confessions is described. Specifically, confessional statements "identify the church as a community known by its convictions as well as by its actions."

The third area of limitation refers to "the government of church." In using this phrase the *Book of Order* makes a significant transition between what we believe about the capital "C" Church and how we go about being the small "c" church.[54] The point is that the *Book of Order* needs to be seen as the fruit of theological reflection. With this phrase the discussion emerges from confessional language about who Jesus is and what he is doing and turns to provisions for guiding the specific fellowship called the Presbyterian Church (U.S.A.).

Wrangling over changes in the *Book of Order* suggests that few Presbyterians have any sense of this connection so forcefully presented in G-1.0100c. Some of our distress as we seek to find our way into the twenty-first century may be that so few of us take this connection seriously, consistent with the vows of ordination for those who are presbyters. We have neglected the taproot that feeds our fellowship, forgetting that our church can prosper only by the blessing of the One who is Lord of the church, including our branch.

In the three designated areas of church life, which amount to much of our life together, line 10 becomes the challenge for the church as it faces new challenges and opportunities. The subject is "matters." Such a simple word describes comprehensively what goes on in the life of the church. This apparently simple word refers not only to what we do, but also to how we go about obeying the Lord of the church universal and our church.

The matters "are to be ordered." Here is a second command, derived from the discussion of lines 5–7, this time in the imperative voice: "are to be."[55] Again, these are three little words of grace and power. The formula that follows is to be taken seriously, as a clear injunction. Perhaps we would be more aware of this command if there were a cross-reference to this as a basis for the ordination vow, "Will you be governed by our church's polity?" (G-14.0207e; G-14.0405b(5)). It seems to me that Presbyterians overuse the word *mandate* in its various forms. This word supposedly conveys some form of power beyond the fact that a governing body has voted for a specific proposal. Here in line 10 is the clearest of all mandates.

In the absence of clear commands from the Lord of the church, believers are to order their community. People who first encounter the *Book of Order* sometimes ask, "Whose order?" The answer, as we have seen in the preceding pages, is: "Our understanding, as Presbyterians, of God's order." We Americans are wary of someone telling us what to do. We consider it an infringement on our freedom.

We Americans have a rich pragmatic tradition. "Whatever works" is a principle embedded in us early as we grow up. Ingenuity has a high value in our society. We have a tendency to invent solutions to our problems that seem wise or effective. Efficiency and "making sense" are deep within our psyches. "Figure it out" is something we hear from our earliest days.

A consequence of this is to assume that fixing what has gone wrong and finding solutions to apparent problems is something anyone can do. That attitude underlies many of the anomalies in church life. For example, reviewing overtures to the General Assembly from presbyteries year after year demonstrates which problems or puzzles have emerged within a presbytery or sometimes a wider area. What is often called "clutter" in our *Book of Order* is the result of putting patches on what didn't seem to work otherwise. The problem with pragmatic solutions is that they are often made irrelevant over time. We might ponder Jesus' parable of the often-patched garment to understand why it is that ad hoc "solutions" are usually temporary.[56]

The direction is modified by the adverbial phrase "according to." The adverb focuses on the "how" of faith as well as the "what." The business of working out how we are to live and work together as a community of faith is a disciplined enterprise. These words alert us to how we should implement the formula expressed in lines 11–13.

The first and foremost element of the formula (line 11) is "the Word," referring to the Word of God. The "whole counsel of God's Word"[57] now enters the process, enlarging the basis beyond the commandments of Jesus Christ for determining how to order our life together. The first impression is that all of Scripture needs to be taken into account as we consider how we should organize ourselves for our service to God. The broader base complicates the process because of the increased amount of material included. The amount of data to be considered is imposing and daunting.

The Directory for Worship corrects our tendency to limit the meaning of *Word* to the Bible. There are several ways in which "the Word" refers to Jesus Christ:

> Jesus Christ is the living God present in common life. The One who is proclaimed in the witness of faith is
> > the Word of God spoken at creation,
> > the Word of God promising and commanding throughout covenant history,
> > the Word of God
> > > who became flesh and dwelt among us,
> > > who was crucified and raised in power,
> > > who shall return in triumph to judge and reign. (W-1.1003c)

Element 1 of the formula recalls how we began, reminding us of the Lord of the church. Clearly, as inheritors of Christ's endowment, we must consider the written Word as the witness to the Living Word.

Such emphasis on "the Word," which has historically characterized Presbyterians, is seriously weakened when knowledge of Scripture among Presbyterians is shown to be weak. Lamenting what some call widespread scriptural illiteracy has led some to solve this problem by stressing how inspired and inerrant the Bible is. Such feuding has continued for nearly a century, with the only result being the continuing decline among Presbyterians of familiarity with the Bible. Unfortunately, while this theological dispute has continued, emphasis on church school education has also declined.

One consequence of this sad history is that disputes in our fellowship seem increasingly to focus on highly selective and abbreviated scriptural references as we seek to deal with emerging issues confronting us. The "whole counsel of God" has been replaced by the merchandising of specific texts which appear to "prove" one side or another.[58] The emphasis has shifted from weighing various texts to citing specific brief passages as authoritative, in an attempt to cut short consideration of additional possibly relevant material. When modern marketing strategies are employed to "sell" selected texts as determinative, the appeal to the "whole counsel" is cut short, and the process is weakened.

"According to the Word" carries with it remembering that Christ's commandment to love one another is paramount. The focus is on the "how" at least as much as on the "what." Truth that comes without the envelope of love is thus contrary to the Word.

Line 12 links the second element, "reason," with the third, "sound judgment." Both terms appear to raise more questions than they resolve. Reason is a concept that has become suspect. Ever since the late eighteenth century when Immanuel Kant introduced the concept of pure reason, the term has been stretched and twisted into something suspicious, amorphous. Yet we still understand what it is to give "reasons" for our views, which is sufficiently helpful for our present purpose.

A reasonable discussion or debate takes place when points of view are presented by participants supported by reasons of various sorts. The focus of a reasonable discussion is the merit of the alternatives, so that a decision may be reached by evaluation of the alternatives. Certain kinds of material are excluded from consideration, such as personal attacks and appeals to competing authority.

Reason within the Christian community must be rooted in the affirmations of faith, so that the self-giving love of the Savior should also characterize our discussions with one another. One need not be in the church for very long to discover that this is one of the most readily forgotten aspects of life together in any fellowship, at whatever level. If we are indeed corporately the body of Christ, angry and divisive discourse wounds the body as much as those who brutalized our Lord on the cross. We have a great deal about which to be humble!

"Sound judgment" is even more challenging. This third component of the formula reminds us that we work in community. On September 20, 1710, the clerk for the Presbytery of Philadelphia, at the conclusion of an apparently lengthy process, introduced presbytery's decision of the matter with the words, "After mature and deliberate Consideration . . ."[59] Our colonial ancestors in the faith hit upon the practice of talking things through as the means of implementing what they understood as "sound judgment."

Jack Rogers, moderator of the 213th General Assembly (2001), reminded many Presbyterians that the model for governing body meetings is found in Acts 15. Early copies of the Form of Government use this passage as the scriptural basis for all four governing bodies.[60] It is distressing that so few meetings of governing bodies understand that this is the model, and that we are seeking to continue this practice in the same spirit.

The final element of the formula, "under the guidance of the Holy Spirit," restates a concern that how Presbyterians determine issues is a matter of faith, that God's Holy Spirit is present in governing body meetings. Perhaps we need to confess that we seldom open ourselves to the possibilities of such a powerful presence. Complaints that such meetings are "just business" reveal that there is an absence of discernment among us.

It has become fashionable for the losing side of a dispute to charge that "they" manipulated the vote. Such allegations carry two unfortunate suppositions: that the commissioners are unable to comprehend what is "really" going on, and are sheep who are easily manipulated by skillful advocates; and that all that is happening is restricted to the here and now, where God's Spirit is unable to guide those seeking God's guidance.

My first experience as a commissioner to General Assembly was in 1976. One issue coming to our committee related to whether the Presbyterian Church (U.S.) should advocate amnesty for those who had evaded the draft for the Vietnam War by going to other countries. On our committee was a retired Marine Corps officer. As we studied and discussed the issue, this gentleman went from vehement opposition to the idea in our first meeting to volunteering to support the committee's recommendation that the proposal be adopted. His explanation of his reversal was a testimony of how his study and prayer had led directly to his decision.

What happened to the colonel can happen to an entire General Assembly. Some whose General Assembly experience extends for decades of careful observation report how each gathering discovers its own spirit or ethos. The virtual impossibility of predicting in advance what that spirit will be or when it will occur has never dampened the hopes of those who whom "GA" is simply another challenge to their political skills. Such politicizing tendencies stand in opposition to this final element in the formula. The ban on absentee ballots in congregational meetings in G-7.0301 is another evidence of this conviction.

"Under the guidance of the Holy Spirit" stands to remind us that more is going on at church meetings than meets the eye. Affirming the sovereignty of God requires a sense that God will direct the church as God will. Attempts to manipulate the outcome, regardless of the motivation or the agenda, always include within themselves an essentially idolatrous attempt to become "as god" regarding one or another decision. That puts one in an awkward position.

Finding Christ

The thirteen lines of G-1.0100c provide the link between our faith and our life together in the Presbyterian Church (U.S.A.). The stance presumes gratitude to God for all we have been given. It reminds us that we are called to demonstrate our gratitude in our witnessing to those around us. We are also challenged, as we engage in this calling, to bear in mind that it is how we are together that also communicates whether it is a holy Lord we serve, or some other lord. What else could be left to say?

Notes

1. During one of the design conferences on Long Island, an attack on a freighter by an enemy submarine was close enough for those present to see and hear the exchange. In order to finance the publication of the series, the Board of Christian Education mortgaged the Philadelphia headquarters in the Witherspoon Building for a million dollars. Some were confident that the sum would never be repaid. They were wrong.

2. William E. Chapman, *History and Theology in the Book of Order: Blood on Every Page* (Louisville, Ky.: Witherspoon Press, 1999), p. 1.

3. During her term as moderator of the 211th General Assembly (1999–2000), Freda Gardner sometimes spoke on this theme in a sermon titled "Mucking Out the Ark."

4. "Church Militant" describes the struggles of the faithful on their way to the Church Triumphant, the communion of saints for eternity. (See *Book of Confessions* C-3.16 and C-5.127–128.)

5. Thus the last sentence of G-2.0200: "'The church reformed, always reforming' according to the Word and the call of the Spirit."

6. For a brief discussion of the process leading up to this decision, read the material in the *Book of Confessions*, p. 252. A more extensive discussion is found beginning on p. xx, where the text of "The Confessional Nature of the Church," adopted by the 209th General Assembly (1997), is reproduced.

7. See Guy S. Klett, ed., *Minutes of the Presbyterian Church in America 1706–1788* (Philadelphia: Presbyterian Historical Society, 1976). The minutes of the Synod of Philadelphia, which met May 23, 1744, begin on p. 193. Those for the Synod of New York for September 16, 1744, begin on p. 263.

8. Ibid., p. 195. I have modernized the spelling and certain abbreviations from the text as printed. Editor Klett inserted the word in brackets as his judgment to clarify the meaning.

9. Ibid., p. 341. This time the bracket is my insertion to cite an earlier remark in unquoted material, for clarity.

10. For example, "An inquirer or candidate shall not undertake to serve a church, even as a temporary supply, without the approval of the presbytery having jurisdiction over the church as well as the approval of the inquirer's or candidate's presbytery."

11. Quoted from the *New Digest*, p. 364, by J. Aspinwall Hodge, in *What Is Presbyterian Law as Defined by the Church Courts?* 8th ed. (Philadelphia: Presbyterian Board of Publication and Sabbath-School Work, 1907), p. 417.

12. Ibid., p. 418. The quotation is identified as from *Presbyterian Digest*, 1886, pp. 442–443.

13. James H. Smylie, *A Brief History of the Presbyterians* (Louisville, Ky.: Geneva Press, 1996), p. 72.

14. Hodge, *What Is Presbyterian Law*, p. 287.

15. Elective affinity courts are "judicatories not bounded by geographical limits, but having a chief regard in their election to diversities of doctrinal belief and ecclesiastical polity." Ibid., page 182.

16. Ibid., p. 287. Regarding the final item, he refers to the *Assembly's Digest*, pp. 656–801, and the *New Digest*, pp. 453–557.

17. See, for example, James H. Moorhead, "The 'Restless Spirit of Radicalism': Old School Fears and the Schism of 1837," in *Journal of Presbyterian History* 78:1 (spring 2000), especially pp. 28–31.

18. Jacob Harris Patton, *A Popular History of the Presbyterian Church in the United States of America* (New York: D. Appleton & Co., 1903), p. 439.

19. Ibid., p. 462.

20. Ibid., p. 472.

21. Bradley J. Longfield, "For Church and Country: The Fundamentalist-Modernist Conflict in the Presbyterian Church," *Journal of Presbyterian History* 78:1 (spring 2000), p. 46. Longfield focuses on the doctrinal dispute, presenting the mission issue as a consequence of the struggle that began in 1910 with the General Assembly's embracing the Five Fundamentals as "essential tenets" for Presbyterians. I am proposing that the unity-mission tension is another perspective, helpful as we seek understanding of the struggles in the early years of the twenty-first century.

22. William Ernest Hocking et al., *Re-Thinking Missions: A Layment's Inquiry After One Hundred Years* (New York: Harper & Brothers, 1932). An analysis of the Hocking Report and its impact is available in John R. Fitzmier and Randall Balmer, "A Poultice for the Bite of the Cobra: The Hocking Report and Presbyterian Missions in the Middle Decades of the Twentieth Century," in Milton J. Coulter, John M. Mulder, and Louis B. Weeks, eds., *The Diversity of Discipleship: The Presbyterians and Twentieth-Century Witness* (Louisville, Ky.: Westminster/ John Knox Press, 1991), pp. 105–125.

23. Quoted in Ned B. Stonehouse, *J. Gresham Machen: A Biographical Memoir* (Grand Rapids: Wm. B. Eerdmans Publishing Co., 1954), pp. 474–475. This volume presents Machen's life and work in a favorable way. Machen cites specific passages in Hocking, which seventy years later sound much less extreme than how he took them. Yet one can appreciate that these perspectives challenged many assumptions about missions then prevalent.

24. Ibid., p. 482.

25. *The Presbyterian Constitution and Digest* (Philadelphia: Office of the General Assembly of the United Presbyterian Church in the United States of America, 1963), vol. 1, p. A1194.

26. Ibid.

27. Ibid., p. A1197.

28. Stonehouse, *J. Gresham Machen*, pp. 495–502. Stonehouse summarizes the subsequent dispute that led the Machen group to change the name of their denomination from "Presbyterian Church of America" to "Orthodox Presbyterian Church."

29. "We see that some form of organization is necessary in all human society to foster the common peace and maintain concord. We see further that in human transactions some procedure is always in effect, which is to be respected in the interests of public decency, and even of humanity itself. This ought especially to be observed in churches, which are best sustained when all things are under a well-ordered constitution, and which without concord become no churches at all." John Calvin, *Institutes of the Christian Religion*, ed. John T. McNeill, trans. Ford Lewis Battles (Philadelphia: Westminster Press, 1960), IV, x, 27, p. 1205.

30. Ibid. The biblical reference is Matthew 20:28.

31. Samuel Miller, *The Ruling Elder* (Dallas, Tex.: Presbyterian Heritage Publications, 1994), p. 3. This is a reprint in pamphlet form of an excerpt from his 1831 book, *An Essay, on the Warrant, Nature and Duties of the Office of the Ruling Elder, in the Presbyterian Church* (New York: Jonathan Leavitt; Boston: Crocker and Brewster, 1831).

32. Ibid., p. 13. The masculine pronoun is used in the original.

33. Resignation from governing body positions is by writing to the stated clerk. These are elected positions and hence differ in kind from the active service discussed in the text. It is also possible to "renounce the jurisdiction of the church," which removes one from all connection from the Presbyterian Church (U.S.A.). This latter option is a gravely significant step and is taken only in the direst circumstances.

34. Miller, *The Ruling Elder*, p. 15.

35. It is ironic that advocates for ecclesiastical populism have repeatedly demeaned the role of elders by alleging that they are dupes in manipulative schemes, thus casting serious aspersions on the integrity and intelligence of those whose votes and voices they are seeking to enroll in their particular causes.

36. The Second Commandment is, "Thou shalt not make unto thee any graven image, or any likeness of any thing that is in heaven above, or that is in the earth beneath, or that is in the water under the earth: thou shalt not bow down thyself to them, nor serve them: for I the Lord thy God am a jealous God, visiting the iniquity of the fathers upon the children unto the third and fourth generation of them that hate me; and shewing mercy unto thousands of them that love me, and keep my commandments" (C-7.217). The format in list form differs from the paragraph format in the *Book of Confessions*.

37. The citation is found at § 3–5 in the *Book of Church Order* (Atlanta: John Knox Press, 1974). The format has been changed from paragraph to list form for publication in this work. Virtually the same list appears in chapter VI, "Of Ordinances in a Particular Church," of *The Constitution of the Presbyterian Church in the United States of America* (Philadelphia: W. W. Woodward, 1815), p. 348.

38. The word *lively*, which appears in G-1.0100d, will be discussed in chapter 4.

39. D-7.0401 for remedial cases and D-11.0402a for disciplinary trials.

40. G-6.0102, last sentence. "These ordained officers differ from other members in function only."

41. As quoted in www.tk421.net/essays/prime.

42. *Minutes of the 1927 General Assembly.* The report is found on pp. 56–86. This quote is from the CD-ROM version of the *Annotated Book of Order, 2001–2002.*

43. In writing this section, I am indebted to Ethelbert Stauffer's article $\alpha\gamma\alpha\pi\alpha\omega$, in Gerhard Kittel, ed., *Theological Dictionary of the New Testament*, vol. 1 (Grand Rapids: Wm. B. Eerdmans Publishing Co., 1964), especially pp. 44–47.

44. From "Works of Love" (1847), translated by Douglas V. Steere, in Robert Bretall, ed., *A Kierkegaard Anthology* (Princeton, N. J.: Princeton University Press, 1947), p. 290.

45. Ibid., p. 291.

46. The Greek word is $\alpha\lambda\lambda\eta\lambda\omega\nu$.

47. Gerhard Lohfink, *Jesus and Community: The Social Dimension of Christian Faith* (Philadelphia: Fortress Press, 1984), p. 99.

48. James Russell Lowell, "Once to Every Man and Nation," hymn 540 in *The Worshipbook* (Philadelphia: Westminster Press, 1970).

49. For a study of the Greek word $\pi\rho\epsilon\sigma\beta\upsilon\varsigma$, see the article in Kittel, *Theological Dictionary*, vol. VI, pp. 651–683.

50. For a study of the Greek word $\epsilon\pi\iota\sigma\kappa\sigma\pi\sigma\varsigma$, see the article by Hermann Beyer in Kittel, *Theological Dictionary*, vol. II, pp. 599–622.

51. John H. Leith, *Assembly at Westminster: Reformed Theology in the Making* (Atlanta: John Knox Press, 1973), p. 111.

52. Ibid.

53. Note the discussion of service in G-1.0100b, line 5, in chapter 2 above.

54. This distinction between capital-letter Church and lowercase church is difficult to apply and is not attempted in our discussion.

55. Note that this form is described in the Preface of the *Book of Order*, where it is defined as meaning "practice that is mandated."

56. Matthew 9:16 and parallels.

57. *Book of Confessions* 6.006 (Westminster Confession). The text is as follows: "The whole counsel of God, concerning all things necessary for his own glory, man's salvation, faith, and life, is either expressly set down in Scripture, or by good and necessary consequence may be deduced from Scripture: unto which nothing at any time is to be added, whether by new revelations of the Spirit, or traditions of men. Nevertheless we acknowledge the inward illumination of the Spirit of God to be necessary for the saving understanding of such things as are revealed in the Word; and that there are some circumstances concerning the worship of God, and government of the Church, common to human actions and societies, which are to be ordered by the light of nature and Christian prudence, according to the general rules of the Word, which are always to be observed."

58. The notion of "proof texts" came into our tradition notably during the Westminster Assembly of 1643 and beyond. The *Book of Confessions* continues to include Scripture references to the Westminster documents as end notes (Confession, Larger and Shorter Catechisms). These reflect the debates of the Assembly, in which much of the discussion revolved around the question of which texts were more persuasive.

    The subsequent notion of "proof-texting" differs from the Westminster process in that specific texts are appealed to as "the" authority, without the balance of alternate texts.

59. Guy S. Klett, ed., *Minutes of the Presbyterian Church in America, 1706–1788* (Philadelphia: Presbyterian Historical Society, 1976), p. 8.

60. The editions of 1815 and 1834 both contain such references.

1. *In affirming with the earliest Christians that Jesus is Lord,*
2.   *the Church confesses that*
3.   *he is its hope and*
4.   *that the Church, as Christ's body,*
5.   *is bound to his authority and*
6.   *thus free to live in the lively, joyous reality*
7.   *of the grace of God.*

(G-1.0100d)

4

Orderly Meditations

The major controversy of the 213th General Assembly (2001) occurred as a dispute over whether the Presbyterian Church (U.S.A.) really held to the lordship of Jesus Christ. Bruising debates over this issue during the Louisville meeting continued to trouble Presbyterians after the General Assembly had adjourned. The question seemed to be, "Does our church believe in the lordship of Jesus Christ?"

The concern arose when previous to the meeting a speaker suggested in a meeting under the auspices of the denomination that perhaps Jesus was not the only savior, questioning the unique role of Jesus Christ as the only savior for humankind. The ensuing panic was for many an attempt to ensure that the risen Christ was indeed acknowledged as "the savior for all men" (C-9.10).

This dispute likely arose as a consequence of the increasing religious diversity in the United States. How are we to speak of our basic understanding of Jesus Christ as our Savior and Lord when our neighbors use different names for divinity and challenge or attack our faith commitment? How do we express our own sense that "in Christ God was reconciling the world to himself" (2 Cor. 5:19)? It is unfortunate that the affirmation in G-1.0100d apparently never surfaced in the discussions during that General Assembly.

Line 1 leaves little doubt regarding where the Presbyterian Church (U.S.A.) stands on who Jesus is, the area of theology traditionally known as Christology. The prepositional phrase in which we find the affirmation reminds us that our affirmation of faith in Jesus Christ is consonant with what was professed by the earliest Christians. This phrase also refers to what the Apostles' Creed calls the "communion of saints" (C-2.3).

In a more contemporary way of speaking, Christ's church is transhistorical. The Christian fellowship includes the faithful of all ages. Often at Communion we remember "the faithful departed," sometimes referring to them as those who have joined the "Church Triumphant." We saw earlier that the Westminster Confession defines the church as "the whole number of the elect, that have been, are, or shall be gathered into one" (C-6.140).[1] While it appears that this paragraph begins with only a backward look, the rest of Westminster's notion of the church will soon appear.

This phrase asserts that we Presbyterians continue in the company of the faithful from the earliest faithful disciples. Paul told the troubled church in Corinth that "no one can confess 'Jesus is Lord,' unless . . . guided by the Holy Spirit" (1 Cor. 12:3f TEV). The function of the confessions we have selected is to "summarize the essence of the Christian tradition" (G-2.0100b).

Entrance into our denomination requires "faith in Jesus Christ as Savior and acceptance of his Lordship in all of life" (G-5.0101a), which is then further qualified as "a public profession of faith in Jesus as Lord." One needs to go on record publicly regarding who Jesus is and what Jesus means for one's life. While that sounds as if it were a complication of the passage from First Corinthians, it is very close to another comment of Paul's in Romans 10:9: "If on your lips is the confession, 'Jesus is Lord,' and in your heart the faith that God raised him from death, you will be saved" (TEV).

The term *lord* is often described as a power term, one that triggers a fear of domination or abuse. There is a medieval ring to the term, a reminder of a social order where relationships were rigid, where status meant power over the lives of those lower in the social pyramid. Older translations follow an ancient Hebrew tradition of not using the name of God, but using a synonym. In English, this appears as "LORD," reminding the reader simultaneously of the need to take care when speaking the name of God (Exod. 20:7; Deut. 5:11), while at the same time affirming God's dealing with creation, and with us as humans.

A contemporary approach is to substitute "sovereign" for "lord." Such a strategy reminds us that Jesus is more than simply a good teacher or an exemplary human being. To say that Jesus is Lord or Sovereign is to assert that Jesus is God. The simple yet ancient three-word expression, which we so often (yet so casually) utter, is itself a witness to the Resurrection, another way of saying that Jesus is divine.

Discussing the confession that "Jesus is Lord," Allan Boesak writes of the Christians to whom the book of Revelation was addressed:

> Because this confession had all kinds of consequences for Christian attitudes toward politics, the emperor, military service, and so forth, Christians came to be regarded more and more as a threat to the security of the state and the welfare of its citizens.[2]

Boesak was writing to his fellow Christians in South Africa at the time, later preaching this same sermon to the 196th General Assembly meeting in Phoenix, Arizona, in 1984.

While the three-word confession is ancient, it is also amazingly ecumenical. This is not a denominational way of speaking, but one that is common to the church universal. The brevity of this affirmation carries with it ambiguity. Some say that the affirmation raises more questions than it answers. That is a given for such a succinct expression of the central understanding of our Christian faith. That these three words continue to function as a simple, yet profound, expression of faith in Jesus Christ into the third millennium after Christ suggests that care in understanding its function is appropriate, and that we should not discard these treasured words out of hand. Adding "little" words, such as "my" or "the," begins the process of qualifying the historic declaration. The result expresses the person's intensity and depth of faith, at the expense of the broader community of believers. When such qualifiers are required in a community of faith, lines are drawn that divide.[3]

More dangerous is the insistence that one group requires that others conform themselves to the specific expression, as if any formulation is required by God. In G-1.0301–.0302, where "conscience" is protected, groups maintain the authority to define terms of admission. "They may, not withstanding, err, in making the terms of communion either too lax or too narrow: yet, even in this case, they do not infringe on the liberty or the rights of others, but only make an improper use of their own." When the *Book of Order* considers matters of faith, one of the distinctive notes is "the recognition of the human tendency to idolatry and tyranny" (G-2.0500a(4)).

To confess Jesus as Lord is to realize how vulnerable we are to wanting to "lord it over" those around us with whom we may disagree. This phrase appears twice in the New Testament (Matt. 20:25; Mark 10:42), where the point is to distinguish how Jesus' followers go about their work from how others may do theirs. Werner Foerster comments: "It is likely that the word implies the tendency towards compulsion or oppression which is immanent in all earthly power."[4] The phrase pointedly reminds us that confessing "Jesus is Lord" commits us to recognizing our own proclivity to "compulsion or oppression." Whenever we give in to these alternate means, regardless of our attempts to justify them, it erodes our professed faith.

Line 1 in a way summarizes the previous three paragraphs. These few words are later rephrased in G-2.0300: "In its confessions, the Presbyterian Church (U.S.A.) gives witness to the faith of the Church catholic." There is, again, an ambiguity in such a statement. On the one hand, Presbyterians stand with many other Christian bodies continuing to witness to the power and purpose of Jesus Christ. On the other hand, that tradition is itself a broad one, with crosscurrents of understandings, of various vocabularies as attempts to express what often seems beyond expression. This apparently simple assertion brings us to a fresh realization that Paul's comment that "we have this treasure in clay jars" (2 Cor. 4:7) refers even to our simplest credo.

Line 2 begins, "the Church confesses . . ." The word *confess* is another ambiguous word for many modern believers. To confess is to own up to something. It is a highly personal form of communication. The Greek word for *confess*, ομολογεω, used in Romans 10, is given three senses in the *Theological Dictionary of the New Testament*[5]:

1. to assure, promise, admit, concede
2. to make a (judicial) statement, to bear witness (in court)
3. to make a solemn statement of faith

There is some ambiguity about this word in English, as we confess our sins on the one hand, and then confess our faith on the other as we worship. The Greek word includes an overtone that confession in any of the senses is the action of a community. It is what we say together that lies at the heart of any confession. There must be social validation for a confession to have validity. Otherwise, one is merely making an assertion.

What is it that the church confesses? The word *that* in line 2, repeated in line 4, indicates that there are two foci for the church's outlook, its stance as it looks toward the future. Since September 11, 2001, we in the United States once again have entered a time when the word *future* has taken on more negative than positive overtones. The historic optimism of the American people has been eroded by terrorism from abroad and evidence of moral erosion within our borders. Personal and corporate misdoings dominate our media. It is as if our nation had flown into a cultural fog without any reliable instruments or guidance.

These two words, "confess that," point to unexpected yet challenging answers to what the church in times such as these is called to confess. The first confession comes in line 3, which declares that the hope of the church is Jesus Christ ("he is its hope").

The verb *is* appears three times in this paragraph. Such a small word tends to be overlooked. In the light of verbs used elsewhere in G-1.0100, this frequency suggests that we are continuing an emphasis on reality from a Christian and Presbyterian point of view. We are reminded that we stand on the firm ground of God's reality, experiences to the contrary notwithstanding.

Many Presbyterians may admit the tendency to consider other predictors, such as membership and financial trends, for the future of the Presbyterian Church (U.S.A.). The surprise on reading line 3 is what is not said: neither doctrine, nor purity, nor program, nor structure, nor budget. Jesus Christ is the hope of the church, even as Christ is Lord of the church. Yet in much of our life together, these are the topics which are often cited as determiners of our church's future. And so they may be. Still, the ultimate hope for every Christian is simply Jesus Christ.

New Testament professor Walter C. Hofheinz suggested how the book of Revelation could be made into a film. The screen would be split; the upper segment would show what was happening in heaven, while the lower area would present what was happening on earth. For example, chapter 4 begins, "After this, I looked, and there in heaven a door stood open," introducing a section taking place in heaven. Chapter 7 begins, "After this I saw four angels standing at the four corners of the earth." Dr. Hofheinz suggested that this linear presentation was intended to portray how both actions were going on simultaneously.[6]

We found in chapter 3 a point at which the church on earth was emphasized. We now find ourselves dealing again with the invisible, eternal church. We have come to another place, even more challenging, where we are called to consider what difference it makes to confess that Jesus Christ is the hope of the church.

It is essential that the affirmation "Christ is our hope" is not forgotten when we deal with doctrine, purity, programs, structures, and budgets. Our hope in Christ is the context within which we are called to determine what we will do next in the church, whether it be in a session, a presbytery, a synod, or a General Assembly. It is easy to become focused on specifics, on whether one specific course of action is likely to enhance our witness and build up our church. Forgetting that Christ is our hope leaves us caught in the net of pragmatism and rhetoric, of seeking to fine-tune what appeals to our sense of "how things work," derived more from our experience than from an awareness that we are engaged in the theological task of translating the Good News of Christ into the specifics of ministry.

Presbyopia is the term for "nearsighted." The Greek roots mean "elder vision." Some of us have heard an eye doctor, after checking our eyes, say, "Your eyes are fine now, but after you reach thirty-five, we will be seeing a lot more of each other." We discover that the choice is often between squinting or glasses.

"Hope in Christ" can be understood as the corrective to fascination with details. We need theological bifocals, so that we may become skilled in seeing both the details and the longer view. Hope in Christ is the long view, the confidence that our times are in God's hands (Ps. 31:15).

This is the message from the believers in Germany during the Hitler regime, from whom came the Theological Declaration of Barmen, which in its penultimate paragraph declares for us:

> We reject the false doctrine, as though the Church in human arrogance could place the Word and work of the Lord in the service of any arbitrarily chosen desires, purposes, and plans. (C-8.27)

A similar appreciation for hope in Christ while surrounded with seemingly insurmountable agony was the witness of Christians in South Africa as they witnessed against apartheid through the last half of the twentieth century. As Boesak wrote, speaking of the history of our planet,

> Christians and the church are part of this history, not simply submerged by events that roll over them like waves from the sea. No, they are in history with responsibility *for* it—to challenge it, change it, undermine it, until it conforms to the norms of the kingdom of God and until the world recognizes the lordship of Jesus the Messiah.[7]

It is evident from this quote that Allan Boesak was writing as an ethicist, not as a biblical commentator or New Testament scholar.

Boesak implicitly rebuts the notion of eschatology sometimes characterized as "pie in the sky in the sweet bye and bye." There is a strong tendency for eschatology to become apocalyptic. This form of literature regards the world as becoming increasingly evil, passing beyond the realm of rescue, assuming that the only "way out" is for God to rescue those who remain faithful. Stripped of their rhetoric, apocalyptics only give hope to themselves. All one can do, according to their view, is to separate from evil and pray.

Boesak articulates an evangelical response that reflects hope in the sovereign God, drawing power from such faith which works with God by grace, seeking God's kingdom by offering a "more excellent way." Boesak is consistent with line 3 of this paragraph, as well as with the challenging expression found later in the *Book of Order*: "The Church of Jesus Christ is the provisional demonstration of what God intends for all of humanity" (G-3.0200). Such a confident attitude toward mission will find further expression in the final line of this paragraph.

A similar position is demonstrated in how the Office of Theology and Worship responded to a request of the 213th General Assembly (2001) for "materials that will help our congregations better understand the theological richness of the Lordship of Jesus Christ"[8] by producing a brief pamphlet, *Hope in the Lord Jesus Christ.*[9] Although the booklet does not refer to G-1.0100d, it does cite numerous passages from Scripture and the *Book of Confessions*.

Line 3 ends with a conjunction, *and*. These three letters are so ordinary that we may be tempted to overlook them, or at least to slide over the meaning. *And* means that what follows is understood to be further development of the point of the phrase, which is the nature of what believing Presbyterians confess as true. The connection between the assertion of hope and what follows shows that they are coordinate, equally important.

The coordinate expression in line 4 reintroduces a concept introduced as the "last word" in G-1.0100a, that is, that the church is Christ's body. The wording we find now is a subordinate clause modifying church, "as Christ's body," reiterating the theme introduced earlier. Elsewhere in the *Book of Order*, this understanding is expanded: "The Church is the body of Christ, both in its corporate life and in the lives of its individual members, and is called to give shape and substance to this truth" (G-3.0200c). Such a comment may come as a surprise in two ways: the requirement that both corporate and personal discipleship need to be consonant with the gospel, and that both the church and its members are called to live out their discipleship in "shape and substance."

Line 5 introduces a paradoxical description of the church with another *is*. The first reality is that the church "is bound to his authority." *Bound* is not a word readily accepted today. We are tempted to skip over this word, with some allusion to our freedom in Christ. Yet here it is, meant to be taken seriously. In fact, the image is biblical, often used by the apostle Paul, who identifies himself as a "prisoner in the Lord" (Eph. 4:1). The Greek word often translated "servant" actually is the word for "slave." When we come to line 6 of this section, we will look more closely at Paul's juxtaposition of *free* and *bound*.

For now, *bound* arises from the confession that Jesus is Lord, the One to whom ultimate loyalty is appropriate, the One to whom all authority is given on heaven and on earth. It means being committed to Jesus Christ as the only true authority in a world awhirl with claims of ultimacy in the name of other "realities." As we confess, we bind ourselves to the entity confessed.

In the mid-twentieth century, loyalty oaths were a major issue. Those who worked for tax-supported entities were often required to sign a pledge that they were not subversive to the government of the United States of America. Some felt that this was an unwarranted intrusion on their freedom of thought. Others felt that they, as Christians, had an ultimate loyalty to Jesus Christ beyond loyalty to our country. There was considerable discussion, much emotion, and major controversy.

At the turn of the millennium, the issue of ultimate authority has become explicitly religious. In our country, there are now millions for whom God's name is different. There appear to be more Muslims than Presbyterians in the United States today. This is in contrast to mid-century, when there was a Presbyterian president and it was said half-seriously that the Presbyterian Church was the Republican Party at prayer.

Things are much different now. There is a new dimension to the traditional phrase "Jesus is Lord." The affirmation so long taken for granted now becomes a choice between live alternative religious faiths, some of whose followers are more numerous than us Presbyterians. Matters of faith become more difficult to determine as challenges from various alternative views become increasingly evident. Evangelism is no longer simply a matter of seeking and finding the unchurched, who are assumed to only need reminding that Jesus is their Savior.

This new situation challenges our self-understanding as a community of faith. How should we as followers of Jesus Christ conduct ourselves when our neighbors' faith commitments have to do with which name of God is acceptable? Recent events have awakened us to what was spoken of fifty years ago as "resurgent Islam."[10] Most of us dismissed such a warning as unlikely, particularly in the light of the mission enterprise of ecumenical Christianity. We now rue our smugness.

Rather than confess our error, we react to "the other" in various ways. We Americans have since 1945 seen the world as a playing field where we are defending our particular way of life. We assumed that we were engaged in a zero-sum game, where the ultimate outcome was seen in terms of whether we had won or lost.[11] We have thus moved in sixty years from identifying our enemy as two countries (Germany and Japan), to an economic system (communism), to a mode of political action (terrorism), to a different religion (Islam). It is not surprising that such competitiveness has infected the way we Presbyterians deal with one another over emerging issues among us.

Few of us have wondered about the possibility of "a more excellent way." Some educators have sought to introduce noncompetitive games as an alternative, with some success. Proponents of this movement acknowledge that progress is slow, given the American fascination with competitive sports, both individual and team varieties.

The mathematician John Nash modified John von Neumann's approach in his 1950 dissertation by introducing a distinction between cooperative and noncooperative games:

> Cooperative games are games in which the players can make enforceable agreements with other players. In other words, as a group they can fully

commit themselves to specific strategies. In contrast, in a noncooperative game, such collective commitment is impossible. There are no enforceable agreements. By broadening the theory to include games that are a mix of cooperation and competition, Nash succeeded in opening the door to applications of game theory to economics, political science, sociology, and ultimately evolutionary biology. [12]

I am suggesting that the metaphor can be expanded to include how we understand our relationships with people of other faiths. This requires that we understand what our faith words mean within our own fellowship, while accepting that not everyone has to use "our" words the same way we do.

Yale theologian George Lindbeck makes a similar point while discussing relationships between faithful people of different faiths.

> The general point is that, provided a religion stresses service rather than domination, it is likely to contribute more to the future of humanity if it preserves its own distinctiveness and integrity than if it yields to the homogenizing tendencies associated with liberal experiential-expressivism.
>
> The conclusion is paradoxical: Religious communities are likely to be practically relevant in the long run to the degree that they do not first ask what is either practical or relevant, but instead concentrate on their own intratextual outlooks and forms of life.[13]

Lindbeck states his position with careful, precise language which has been honed by years of dialogue between Christian denominations, as well as with people of other faiths. His sophisticated vocabulary expresses a position consistent with implications of John Nash's insight from the field of mathematics.

Lindbeck's position is a sophisticated appeal for what I call our need for humility. The apostle Paul understood that "we have this treasure in clay jars" (2 Cor. 4:7). Our highest thoughts, our deepest commitment, our most careful language, by definition fall far short of expressing the fullness of God's intention for all humanity. Our human condition is such that what we know about God is always a gift from God, however it comes. Similarly, our expressions about God use what language we know, which becomes our witness by God's grace. At the same time, our way of witness always falls short of being "determinative," as we are mindful of who God is. To lose the sense of mystery, the distance between the holy God who gives us what knowledge we have of God, is to forget ourselves in God's holy Presence.

As if to remind us of whose we are, line 5 uses the word *authority*, a word that has unfortunately become a synonym for *power*. One indication of our culture's fascination with power is this inability to distinguish between legitimate power and power sought for and wielded for its own sake. *Authority* has the deeper sense discussed in chapter 1. That the term emerges again at the end of the section underlines its significance.

Line 6 of this final paragraph may come as a surprise to many. The Presbyterian reputation derived from the dour Scots heritage has persisted to the present. Presbyterian hymns were in the past known as "old Scotch groaners." Presbyterian worship has been characterized by its order and solemnity.

The story is told of a boy who, during a Presbyterian service, was whispering to his mother. She kept asking him to be quiet. Eventually, the mother sat him up straight in the pew in a way that conveyed her serious intent. The boy's response was to begin whimpering, with tears coming from his eyes. The mother's quiet response to this new behavior was, "There, now. That's better."

We wince at this story for several reasons. Not only would this form of reproof be frowned upon today. At the same time, there have been occasions when such apparent support of sad quiet was considered the norm for worship in our tradition.

Now we read, in the *Book of Order*, the other half of the paradox of these lines. After commitment, freedom! One of the blessings of living in the United States of America is the sense of freedom we have. We come to assume that we are free to do as we please. Our national Constitution enshrines in the first ten amendments numerous freedoms we take as our rights as citizens. But in this context it is not freedom understood politically, but theologically.

In the *Book of Order*, it would be better to turn to 1 Corinthians 9 as an exposition of what freedom in the present context is meant to convey. Paul struggles with the dilemma of freedom that the Corinthians apparently claimed as justification for their behavior. His response to their charges is that he has not claimed his "rights" as an expression of his freedom. Paul asserts, "For though I am free with respect to all, I have made myself a slave to all, that I might win more of them" (1 Cor. 9:19). Freedom means the freedom to go the second mile, to do more than is required or expected, "for the sake of the gospel" (v. 23).

Freedom in Christ is only possible when we are bound to Christ's authority in a way consonant with how Christ exercises the immense authority he has received. We proclaim that Christ "emptied himself, taking the form of a servant" (Phil. 2:6–7; NRSV slave). Our proclamation resonates by demonstrating that we have learned to do the same. We Presbyterians love to advocate even more than to debate. There is peril in advocacy when it goes beyond Paul's reminder that "[love] does not insist on its own way" (1 Cor. 13:5). Our history since the early eighteenth century suggests that we have consistently tripped over, and thus eroded, the force of our proclamation of the Good News.

Line 6 points to how we are to live. Three words that describe faithful living are emphasized in this line: lively, joyous, and reality. Each of these words bears reflection. *Lively* is not a word usually associated with Presbyterians. Our concern for order seems contrary to liveliness. Thus, we have another paradox, where appar-ent contradiction finds resolution in following as disciples of Jesus Christ. That "lively" is rarely seen as characterizing Presbyterians is evidence that we have fallen short of this hope.

Within our tradition, there has been an evident fear of liveliness. We recognize that resistance to change has often been a prominent identifier of Presbyterians. Appreciation for our tradition has turned us to the past as if we were curators of precious relics, rather than stewards of the Good News which Jesus characterized as new wine whose bubbles have a way of bursting old wineskins, or a patch on old cloth that produces a bigger tear (Mark 2:22). While balance is certainly necessary, not to mention our impoverished understanding of our tradition, we need to admit our addiction to nostalgia, so that we may begin to appreciate newness as a sign of life.

The *Book of Order*, which we inherited with reunion in 1983, explicitly reminded us that diversity was inherent in our faith. We are called as a matter of faith to "a new openness" in four specific areas of our mission (G-3.0401). The first of these (G-3.0401a) gives a commentary on this word *lively*:

> The Church is called to a new openness to the presence of God in the Church and in the world, to more fundamental obedience, and to a more joyous celebration in worship and work.

We would do well to spend considerable time on how this affects our lives together. Governing bodies would find plenty to challenge the objection that "we have never done it that way."

In chapter 4 there is a section entitled "Diversity and Inclusiveness" (G-4.0400). Our history since 1983 has been one where increasing diversity has become a major component of our membership. While to some extent it mirrors changes in the population of our country, diversity is also the fruit of our mission enterprise, planting Presbyterian churches around the world. One evidence of this new situation was the 1999 amendment, adding G-11.0404f, which enables presbyteries to enroll a new immigrant pastor when a presbytery "determines that its strategy for mission with that constituency requires it." This provision is a step of faithfulness to foster liveliness.

Diversity of membership has brought liveliness to us in other ways. One noteworthy example is in worship, particularly in the language of worship. Many Presbyterians are startled when they find that the Directory for Worship says appropriate language

a. is more expressive than rationalistic,
b. builds up and persuades as well as informs and describes,
c. creates ardor as well as order,
d. is the utterance of the whole community of faith as well as the devotion of individuals. (W-1.2005)

These words stand as a challenge to many of the traditional limits placed on language in worship. The increasingly diverse constituency carries with it the rediscovery of how these characteristics, adopted in 1988, liberate worship to find new patterns.

Diversity is even more clearly emphasized in W-1.2006. The first of the two paragraphs warns against language that would "exclude the expression of diverse cultures . . . or deny emerging needs and identities of believers." The following paragraph is an even stronger setting forth of the implications of diversity:

> The church shall strive in its worship to use language about God which is intentionally as diverse and varied as the Bible and our theological traditions. The church is committed to using language in such a way that all members of the community of faith may recognize themselves to be included, addressed, and equally cherished before God. Seeking to bear witness to the whole world, the church struggles to use language which is faithful to biblical truth and which neither purposely nor inadvertently excludes people because of gender, color, or other circumstance in life.

Again, governing bodies are asked to review their traditional practices in the light of the strong verb "shall strive." The phrasing recognizes the challenge implicit in this provision, as well as the need for reexamination of how we traditionally go about our worship services.

The second surprising word in line 6 of the paragraph is *joyous*, which is a synonym for "lively" as shown in the above reference to G-3.0401a. The text for the hymn "Joyful, Joyful We Adore Thee," set to the theme of the final movement of Beethoven's Ninth (Choral) Symphony, was written by noted Presbyterian pastor Henry van Dyke in 1907. Beethoven had used Schiller's text "Ode to Joy" ("An die Freude" in German) as the culmination of this symphony. Van Dyke took the focus and provided a text expressing the joy of the Christian.

Joy for the Christian is a result of commitment to Christ. There is a profound "peace that passes understanding" from which songs and poetry spring in praise to God. It is more than elation at triumph or victory. Joy is not "just another emotion," but a sense of relief derived from being reconciled to God in Jesus Christ. Songs of joy are better than any prose.

The last word of line 6 is "reality." The final fruit of commitment to Christ's authority is the ability to look at reality full on. Paul's paean of praise in Romans 8 provides the basis for this assertion. Nothing can separate us from God's love in Christ Jesus (vv. 38–39). Knowing that Jesus is Lord in the fullness of that expression enables the faithful disciple to look directly at reality and to deal with whatever comes, confidently and assuredly. Of course, there is anguish and pain. To endure or witness suffering grips us deeply, sometimes moving us to cry out with the psalmist in lament over what injustice is borne by our brothers and sisters. Yet we can afford to look such evil in the face, confident that God in Christ goes with us always through the darkest valleys of human experience.

Near the end of the *Book of Order*, chapter 2 of the Form of Government, there is a listing of four "great themes of the Reformed tradition" derived from the central affirmation of God's sovereignty. The fourth of these demonstrates the Reformed perspective on reality consistent with the tone of the paragraph under discussion:

The recognition of the human tendency to idolatry and tyranny, which calls the people of God to work for the transformation of society by seeking justice and living in obedience to the Word of God. (G-2.0500a(4))[14]

We find a paradox, looking realistically at two of humankind's major tendencies to sin in a way that empowers relevant mission to the world in which we live "in obedience to the Word of God."

How can we live in such a "tensive relationship"?[15] The "impossible possibility" of the Good News comes when the final line revisits God, the basis of our faith. It is only by God's grace through Jesus Christ that there is a church, and that we are members of it, heirs of God's grace. What Martin Luther and myriad saints have grasped is how we press on. One final time comes the reminder that Christian life is bifocal, and a Christian goes through life seeing both the nuts and bolts of life many assume is all there is, while also being aware of that ineffable dimension beyond sight and touch.

Through Christ, God has endowed humanity with the gift of grace, opening the door to the fullness of life in God's eternal kingdom. As we commit ourselves to Jesus as Lord, we are free to hope whatever comes our way. We Presbyterians thus traditionally celebrate by singing:

Praise God, from whom all blessings flow;
Praise Christ, all people here below;
Praise Holy Spirit evermore;
Praise Triune God, whom we adore. Amen.[16]

Notes

1. See chapter 1.

2. Allan A. Boesak, *Comfort and Protest: Reflections on the Apocalypse of John of Patmos.* (Philadelphia: Westminster Press, 1987), pp. 21–22.

3. The 213th General Assembly (2001) received three overtures (01-43, 01-51, 01-52) requesting acknowledgment in various ways that "Jesus Christ, as he is proclaimed in Holy Scripture, is the only Savior of humanity and the world" (Overture 01-51, *Minutes of the 213th General Assembly (2001)*, Part I, *Journal*, p. 464). The response of the General Assembly to these overtures was an affirmation: "We confess the unique authority of Jesus Christ as Lord. Jesus Christ is also uniquely Savior" (ibid., p. 37).

4. Gerhard Kittel, ed., *Theological Dictionary of the New Testament*, vol. 2 (Grand Rapids: Wm. B. Eerdmans Publishing Co., 1964), p. 575.

5. Kittel, *Theological Dictionary*, vol. 5, pp. 207–208.

6. The suggestion was made in a discussion in the Religion Department of McMurray College, Abilene, Texas, when we both were serving there. Dr. Hofheinz died in the late 1970s.

7. Boesak, *Comfort and Protest*, p. 29.

8. *Minutes of the 213th General Assembly (2001)*, Part I, *Journal*, p. 37.

9. *Hope in the Lord Jesus Christ* (pamphlet) (Louisville, Ky.: Office of Theology and Worship, Presbyterian Church (U.S.A.), 2002). Text, 14 pages; study guide, 9 pages; liturgy, 3 pages. PDS #70-420-02-004.

10. Lecture by Professor Edward Jurji at Princeton Theological Seminary sometime between 1955 and 1958.

11. This phrase comes from the work of John von Neumann's 1928 paper which led to his book written with his Princeton colleague Oskar Morgenstern, *The Theory of Games and Economic Behavior*. A discussion of this development can be found in Sylvia Nasar, *A Beautiful Mind* (New York: Touchstone Books, 1998), pp. 79–92.

12. Ibid., p. 96.

13. George Lindbeck, *The Nature of Doctrine: Religion and Theology in a Postliberal Age* (Philadelphia: Westminster Press, 1984), p. 128.

14. The other three "great themes" in G-2.0500a are: (1) The election of the people of God for service as well as for salvation; (2) Covenant life marked by a disciplined concern for order in the church according to the Word of God; (3) A faithful stewardship that shuns ostentation and seeks proper use of the gifts of God's creation.

15. This phrase comes from Amy Plantinga Pauw, "Attending to the Gaps between Beliefs and Practices," in Miroslav Volf and Dorothy C. Bass, ed., *Practicing Theology: Beliefs and Practices in Christian Life* (Grand Rapids: Wm. B. Eerdmans Publishing Co., 2002), p. 37.

16. Wording by Neil Weatherhogg, *The Presbyterian Hymnal* (Louisville, Ky.: Westminster/John Knox Press, 1990), no. 591.

Appendix
Origins of G-1.0100

The present text of section G-1.0100 of the Form of Government emerged at the time of the reunion of the Presbyterian Church in the United States and the United Presbyterian Church in the United States of America in 1983. Two questions may be asked: Has there always been such an introduction? and What were the sources of this material? This appendix provides background information on these questions.

In an 1815 copy of *The Constitution of the Presbyterian Church in the United States of America*, the Introduction to the Form of Government opens as follows:

> The Synod of *New-York* and *Philadelphia, judging it expedient to ascertain and fix* the system of union, and form of *Government* and *Discipline of the Presbyterian Church in these United States*, under their care; have thought proper to lay down, by way of introduction, a few of the general principles by which they have been hitherto governed, and which are the ground work for the following plan. This, it is hoped, will, in some measure, prevent those rash misconceptions, and uncandid reflections, which usually proceed from an imperfect view of any subject; as well as make the several parts of the system plain, and the whole plan perspicuous and fully understood.[1]

The rest of the Introduction is what we now call the Historic Principles of Church Order (G-1.0300), which opens, "The Synod are unanimously of the opinion . . . "

Chapter 1 of the 1815 Form of Government, "Of the Church," begins, "Jesus Christ, who is now exalted, far above all principality, and power,[a] hath erected, in this world, a kingdom, which is his church."[b] Scripture references for this assertion are:

[a] Ephesians 1:20, 21 and Psalm 68:18.
[b] Psalm 2:6 and Ephesians 1:22, 23.

By 1834 the Preliminary Principles had become Chapter 1, apparently because of amendments approved by the General Assembly in 1821 and 1833.[2]

A Preface was added to the *Book of Church Order* of the Presbyterian Church in the United States in 1961, following a six-year revision process. This preface appears to have served as one source for G-1.0100 in the *Book of Order* at reunion in 1983.

The text of this Preface is as follows:
[Note that **bold** text indicates text included in the 1983 revision for the reunited text; *italicized bold* text indicates minor changes, such as tense of verbs.]

Jesus Christ, upon whose shoulders the government is, whose name is called Wonderful, Counsellor, the Mighty God, the Everlasting Father, the Prince of Peace, of the increase of whose government and peace there shall be no end, sits upon the throne of David, and upon his kingdom to order it and establish it with judgment and with justice henceforth even forever. (Isaiah 9:6–7)

All power is given unto him in heaven and in earth by the Father, who raised him from the dead, and set him on his own right hand, far **above all** principality and power, and might, and dominion, **and every name that is named, not only in this** world, **but also in that which is to come.** The Father **has put all things under** his feet and gave him to be Head over all things to the Church, which is his body, the fullness of him that filleth all in all. (Ephesians 1:20–23)

Jesus Christ, being ascended up far above all heavens, that he might fill all things, received gifts for his Church, and gave officers necessary for the edification of the Church and the perfecting of his saints. (Ephesians 4:10–12)

Jesus Christ, who is the Mediator, the sole Priest, Prophet, King, Savior, and **Head of the Church**, contains in himself all the offices in his Church, and has many of their names attributed to him in the Scriptures. He is Apostle, Teacher, Pastor, Minister, and Bishop, the only Lawgiver in Zion. Since his ascension he is present with his Church by his Spirit and Word, and the benefits of all of his offices are effectually applied by the Holy Spirit.

It belongs to his Majesty from his throne of glory, to rule and teach the Church, through his Spirit and Word, by the ministry of men, thus mediately exercising his own authority, and enforcing his own laws, unto the edification and establishment of his kingdom.

Christ, as King and Head of the Church, has *given* **to his Church its officers**, oracles, **and ordinances.** He has ordained therein his system of doctrine, government, discipline, and worship. These are either expressly set down in Scripture or may by good and necessary inference be deduced therefrom. **In** matters of **the worship of God and the government of the Church**, there are some circumstances common to human actions and societies, which **are ordered by reason** and Christian prudence, **according to the** general rules of the **Word**, which always *are to be* observed. Insofar as this system is expressly set forth in Scripture nothing may be added or taken away.[3]

The other primary source for G-1.0100 is the following material from two chapters of *The Book of Order of the United Presbyterian Church in the United States of America*. From chapter II, 32.01–03:

1. Jesus Christ, having **all power given** unto him in heaven and in earth by the Father, **is head over all things to the Church, which is his body.**

2. Since his ascension to heaven he is present with and governs the Church through his *Word and Spirit*, and *by the ministry of men and women*: thus mediately exercising his authority unto the establishment of his Kingdom.

3. The Lord Jesus **Christ** as the only head of the Church *has given* it the ministry, and the oracles and ordinances of God.[4]

And from chapter III, 33.01–03:

1. Jesus Christ, who is now exalted far above all principality and power, has erected in this world a Kingdom which is his Church, and which is one and the same in all ages.

2. The universal Church consists of all those persons, in every nation, together with their children, who make profession of the holy religion of Christ and submission to his laws.

3. As this immense multitude cannot meet together in one place to hold communion, or to worship God, it is reasonable and warranted by Scripture that they should be divided into many particular churches.[5]

These antecedents suggest possible influences in the composition of G-1.0100. But what did the drafting committee have in mind in proposing this introduction to the *Book of Order* for the newly reunited church? Mr. Robert Adcock, a member of the drafting committee, reported to me that his impression was that the group felt that there needed to be an introductory section. He also found, in notes he took in 1981, that four considerations led to the writing of these paragraphs:

1. That the paragraphs were composed from earlier sources.

2. That the paragraphs expanded on current understandings of Jesus Christ as Lord of the Church.

3. That the paragraphs expressed basic Reformed faith as the committee understood it.

4. That the paragraphs might become a confession of faith useful to the church.[6]

Mr. Adcock and I talked as I was completing the manuscript. The four points from his notebook confirmed hunches that emerged while I was working through these four paragraphs. On the one hand, appreciation grew as the scope and power of the paragraphs dawned on me. At the same time, it was increasingly evident that this introductory section had been overlooked by many in our fellowship.

As we approach the twentieth anniversary of reunion, I hope that the time has come for Presbyterians to appreciate the labor of the committee that crafted a *Book of Order* for the 1983 reunited Presbyterian Church. How delightful the prospect of discovering that what many have been seeking for so long has been there all along, waiting to be "discovered."

Notes

1. (Philadelphia: W. W. Woodward, 1815), p. Ff 2. The one volume contained the [Westminster] Confession of Faith, the Larger Catechism, the Shorter Catechism, the Form of Government, Forms of Process (now called Rules of Discipline), and Directory of Worship, a total of 424 pages, 6 3/4 by 4 1/4 inches. Scripture references are included for all sections.

2. *Constitution* [of the Presbyterian Church in the United States of America] (Philadelphia: Alex. Towar, 1834).

3. *The Book of Church Order of the Presbyterian Church in the United States* (Atlanta: John Knox Press, 1964), "Preface, I, The Form of Government, pp. 19–20.

4. *The Constitution of the United Presbyterian Church in the United States of America*, Part II, *Book of Order* (New York: The Office of the General Assembly of the United Presbyterian Church in the United States of America, 1967) (updated through 1980), chapter II, 32.01–.03.

5. Ibid., chapter III, 33.01–.03. This chapter has two more sections: 33.04 contains the Great Ends of the Church, and 33.05 endorses ecumenical expression through cooperation.

6. Telephone conversation with Robert Adcock, August 1, 2002.

Index of Scripture References

Index of *Book of Confessions*

Index of *Book of Order*

(other than G-1.0100)

Index of General Sources